There's a Treasure in Your Attic

Tammie Rizan

PublishAmerica
Baltimore

First printing

ISBN: 1-4137-6199-2
PUBLISHED BY PUBLISHAMERICA, LLLP
www.publishamerica.com
Baltimore

Printed in the United States of America

This book is dedicated to my children: Kasie, Christopher, Aryka and my sweet baby boy, whom I will see in Heaven someday—Ashlee. Thank you for giving me the courage to realize that life is given so that we may live it to its fullest without reservation, all the while helping one another and giving of ourselves in complete love.

I would like to thank God first and foremost, for giving me the privilege of life and for saving me; my sister, for the encouragement that I can do anything; James, for believing in me, I did it!

I thank my mother and my stepfather for that "Get up, go on, no time to feel sorry for yourself, you can do it" attitude. To all the people who were and are instrumental in my survival of life,
thank you!

Introduction

How many times have you reached out to be loved only to have your hand slapped as if you were stealing from a cookie jar ten minutes before dinner? How many times have you given out love only to have your heart trampled on and beat down as if it were a piece of garbage being tossed out? You tried to be loved by the people you thought were most important in your life, but it didn't matter how much you tried to "get" them to love you, it just never worked. Trapped in a vicious cycle you run, trying not to care, shoving your feelings deep inside of you, convincing yourself that it doesn't matter and that you really don't care. But—you do, that is why the pain is so great. You cry out and scream within yourself, saying it's not fair, and all the while you find yourself in situation after situation that brings more pain, more confusion and more desperation. You snap—feeling as if you can't breathe; you just know you're going to die because, after all, how could any one person endure so much pain. STOP! STOP! You fall into a pool of tears and begin to contemplate ending your life. The one situation, the one problem, the one crisis, finally, this is it. You have no one, nothing, and all that you ever loved is being ripped from the inside to the outside of you. You can't go on, you're at the end of your rope, the end of yourself, and the end of life as you know it. What are you going to do? Give up? Fight? Die? A decision needs to be made, what will it be?

This, my friend, is the time you close your eyes, black out the world, and call upon the name of Jesus. Trust me when I tell you that this is the only thing that can rescue you at this point in your life. You may be asking, "How do you know?" Tell me what your problem is. A distant parent perhaps? Does it appear to you that a parent has no love for you? Did a parent or parents abandon you? Are you a victim of sexual abuse? Maybe you've had to live with someone who drinks a lot, an alcoholic? Did you lose custody of a child? Have you or are you facing physical problems such as cancer or some uncommon disease? Maybe you've been, or are, a victim of verbal and/or physical abuse? What about the death of a child or children? You ask, "How could you possibly know what I'm going through?" I know. The list of questions I just asked you, I have faced and overcome every one of them. How? I know a man named Jesus, who chose me from the foundations of the earth to be His child. Even though I have gone through trials due to Satan, man, and myself, He has kept His hand upon me. He brought me to this point so that I may reach out and help you. You have to understand, my life is not my own, it belongs to Jesus Christ. All of these things I have gone through in my life have made me who I am. I could have chosen to be bitter and place blame on others. Believe me, there were many moments of "passing blame," but the key is to forgive quickly and repent immediately. Sometimes this is easier said than done, I realize that. This is why we need help from God. Even though my own circumstances, and the circumstances of others, caused a lot of my pain, God has shown me that I have the power to choose. Instead of ending up in a gutter depending on drugs, alcohol or some other form of immoral power to lean on, I chose to pick myself up and learn from the trials. I chose to pull out the gold and use it for the glory of God. I call these "trials" character-building lessons. They hurt, yes, but you, not God, determine how long you stay in the fire. God has blessed me tremendously with great treasures on this earth, such as love, hope, peace, and perseverance that will stand until His return or until He calls me home, whichever comes first. My point: God loves you and He wants to help you through the fire. Will you let Him?

In an effort to help others realize how truly wonderful and loved they are in the sight of our precious God, I give you glimpses of a life that some may say is filled with scars and excruciating pain. I won't even pretend that that was not how it was at points in my life. Keep in mind that *was* is the key word here. You can be sure that I was questioning God and all the while rebelling because of what I thought was His ever-present punishment and lack of love for me. I was convinced that every bad thing happening to me was punishment for something I had done to displease Him. Running seemed the only way to get away from Him. The more I ran the more distant He became in my heart, but at the same time, He was annoyingly "in my face." I realize that this seems to be an oxymoron. As I tell you my testimony, my hope is that you can grasp some small part and allow it to touch your heart with the love that our wonderful Savior has filled me with. My prayer is that you will be able to see and overcome the fears and insecurities that Satan has placed within your mind and heart, and allow God's love to flush them away. Please understand that these trials were conquered only because Jesus Christ is my Lord and Savior. He alone has and continues to refine me. This, my friend, is a hazard of being "chosen," but I wouldn't have it any other way. I am who I am because of what Christ brought me through, and what He did for me. Even when I couldn't or didn't want to see or feel His presence, He waited. He was there all the time.

"There's a Treasure in Your Attic"

I lay in bed praying to my God above.
He is the answer to all my questions, the rescuer for every time I fall.
My heart is so heavy from life gone by; as I reflect we talk.
Who else would know better the extent of my joys and my pain?
He gently nudges my mind and waits until I stop acknowledging the time.
It's late and I'm tired.
My mind tries to drift into the lull of sleep.
He continues to gently speak and always gives me revelation at what I think
is an inconvenient time, and yes, sometimes I whine.
He speaks to my soul, and I realize the tiredness my body feels begins to fade.
My heart's ear is persuaded by God's voice.
I hear and feel what He is saying to me.
As in days of old a story is told to make me see what He sees and believes in me.
"A treasure in the attic" are the words I hear.
As I question His Meaning, this is what He explains to me:
"Your mind is like an attic of a home that you've lived in for so long.
Your life experiences are stored here; some are placed ever

so gently in precise order,
on the floor, hanging from the ceiling in plain view, or leaning up against a wall.
Some are thrown in piles and tossed about without a care at all.
There are those that are hidden in dark places, in boxes,
locked in heavy trunks with chains,
or under piles of garbage, never to be seen or felt again.
You live your life doing fine, so you think, as you continue to push, shove,
and hide things in the attic.
It becomes a dark, ugly, and frightening place to be,
a place of lost hope and despair.
It becomes unbearable; you can't put anything else in the attic.
What shall you do?
Leave everything in the attic and continue to live,
knowing that it is collecting dust as it rots, is broken or distraught,
fading away into the darkness?
Let's clean it up, organize it, and search for the treasure in your attic," He says.
As He takes me down this road in my mind's eye, I protest and begin to cry.
He reaches out His hand and says, "Take it; hold on tight, I promise, you'll be fine."
We begin to go through the garbage and junk,
and I see a light trying to push faintly through a window.
I work toward the light, sifting through broken glass, jagged picture frames,
rusty nails, broken furniture, faded pictures, moth-eaten clothing,

and dried up brittle letters from long ago.
The path begins to clear, and as I walk closer to the window I see the cobwebs,
the dust, the dirt, and the filth that has gathered the panes,
trying to drown out the light.
It refuses to give up, and it pushes a beam through the smallest of crevices
demanding to make its presence known,
no matter how subtle it may appear to the darkness around.
I pick up a piece of sackcloth and begin to wipe the glass
until the light is so bright that it blinds me.
I fall to my knees, my face begging to touch the floor.
The warmth from the light touches my back; I feel heat running through my body.
The explanation eludes me,
as I feel empowered with confidence and strength running through my veins.
My blood feels like it has been heated to the boiling point.
I stand to my feet and turn to face my attic.
It was illuminated, exposing all.
I inhale deeply and look around, the silence more than I could bear.
Suddenly I hear a whisper coming from the depths of my soul:
"There's a treasure in your attic."
Among the broken glass, the jagged picture frames, rusty nails,
broken furniture, faded pictures, moth-eaten clothing,
dried up brittle letters from long ago, the dust, the dirt, the cobwebs, and the filth,
a prism of rainbow-colored light catches my eye.
I walk toward it and begin to pull away the garbage that has

cluttered and hid its path.
I remove the junk that was stuck to the object; an image begins to emerge.
I fall to my knees, sobbing uncontrollably.
As I stare into that mirror, I feel a gentle touch on my shoulder and He said to me:
"You are the treasure in the attic."

—Tammie K. Rizan

Satan was lurking, waiting to make a move. You could describe it as lambs in the field, wolves were waiting for a vulnerable moment, a time of weakness, and then they close in...

Lying awake in the darkness, listening intently for any sound that would disturb the night, I prayed fervently that I would not hear familiar footsteps coming my way. The silence is comforting, yet disturbing as I lie in fear. Just when I think this night is safe, I drift into troubled sleep. I am awakened abruptly as I feel his hands touch my body. I pretend to be asleep as I pull the covers tight around my neck and clinch my legs together, hoping that he will go away. I begin to cry and scream inside as he pries my legs apart. Whether vocally or silently, loud or soft, he ignores my pleas. When he is done doing whatever he chose to do on *this* night, he leaves my bed and returns to his. I smell the smoke from his cigarette as I lay there soiled with his fluids and smell. I want to vomit! As I lay there crying, afraid to go clean up, silence fills the room, he drifts into a dementedly peaceful sleep as I drift into a prayer begging for death. This is my life, this is my hell and it began at age nine.

At this tender age, in spite of Satan, God would lay the groundwork for the very salvation of my life. He would reveal Himself to me in such ways that I couldn't deny who He was and is. I know that if He had not given me what I call supernatural experiences, I wouldn't have survived. Being so young, I didn't realize at that time, or any time soon after, the call that was on my life. It wasn't until I was an adult with a family of my own that things became clear to me. However, at this young age, seeds were being planted in my heart that would ultimately become the road to my future with Christ. Oh the paths that I did take, as well as those directed by people I should not have been following. You have to know, as you read, that even though it looks really bad, and yes my confusion far outweighs any sanity, if you will, my life will testify that in the end, and through it all, God had every intention of saving me, and He did.

When I was eight years old, life was so innocent, there were no worries. Life had not yet left its mark of pain and cruelty. The first time God revealed Himself to me, my dad was preaching revival in a storefront; he was a powerful preacher. People would come from all over and pack the building during revival, wherever he was preaching. He gave the altar call and my sister, nine years old at the time, went forward. I remember watching her kneel down to pray, but as I looked up, I saw Jesus walking toward me in robes that were so white they were almost blinding. His feet didn't touch the ground as He walked, and His face was aglow. I couldn't make out His features, but I could tell He was smiling at me. I wasn't afraid; peace and warmth completely surrounded my body and mind. When I looked up at Him, He reached out His hand for me, and I reached back. It was like no one else was in the room, just Jesus and me. The feeling was so awesome, that even to this day, it is indescribable. This was the first of many times I would experience God in such a very real way.

This "vision," if you will, would literally save me. Throughout my life the feeling I felt that day was one that I would search for, for many years to come. When the abuse started at age nine and through many, many trials that followed, I would search for what God had given me at that tender age. Life would literally try to blind me and circumstances couldn't have been crueler. However, the light was there, it was up to me to find it.

By the age of ten, my world would completely unravel. My parents announced in a whirlwind of hostility that they were getting a divorce. It wasn't pretty, as I'm sure you can imagine. However, it was no surprise considering this was the outcome due to previous circumstances. Unfaithfulness was a common practice for my dad. He was a womanizer, all in the name of Christ. He would have sex with women in the churches where he preached. He had absolutely no scruples; he would do it right under their husbands' noses in their own homes, all the while telling everyone he was praying with them. If this weren't bad enough, he would quote scripture while he was molesting others. All the while, he was hiding behind the church. Yes, it seemed to be the end of life as I knew it, and it was. Satan seemed to be winning and there was nothing I could do about it. My life seemed like a bad dream that would never end. It would go from bad to worse with no end in sight. Darkness continued to fall on our family and Satan made his move with a power so forceful that I thought I would surely die. My world was trembling as if an earthquake had come and would not leave.

My trust in God was coming to a painful halt, for you see, the father whom He gave me on this earth was the one abusing me. My trust was shattered and my self-worth was as low as it could get. I felt that no one could protect or help me. If God couldn't then who could? Surely He had abandoned me, what other answer could there be? This father whom God gave me was a minister of the gospel, specifically chosen by Him. I felt betrayed by both. There are those who have asked why I didn't tell someone. Who was I going to tell? No one would believe me, are you kidding? A child verses "a man of God." My dad confirmed this when he told me that if I said anything, he would "blow his brains out," and that I wouldn't have anyone to take care of me. This put a great deal of fear into me. At the time he told me this, my mom had already moved away to another state, so in my mind he was right. He also said it would be my fault and that everyone would blame me. Talk about pressure! So, I said nothing. For years I said nothing. I felt lost most of the time. How could a God who supposedly loved me allow this to happen? I was confused to say the least. I desperately wanted my dad to love me in a "normal" way, and I wanted God to love me, too. My life seemed to be a total mess with no way out. I remember many nights praying that God would just let me die. If He didn't love me, then why let me live? It hurt too much—just let me die!

It seemed that my life would take yet another turn for disaster. I was becoming increasingly ill with a life-threatening disease called Bronchiectasis, a disease that usually afflicted people in their sixties. I would get fevers that would shoot up to 104 or 105 degrees in the evening, and the next morning it would be gone. I would catch the bus and go to school like nothing ever happened. This went on for about four years, from the time I was eleven through fifteen. In the fourth year of this illness, things began to progress for the worst. I remember running or getting nervous, causing me to be short of breath. I would begin to cough and feel like I was choking, as blood would literally come from my lungs. Yes, I was taken to the doctor, but only once. I would find out at the age of fifteen that I was literally on the brink of death.

I remember sitting in Algebra class getting ready to take a test when I began to get nervous, started to sweat, thus causing me to begin coughing. I remember thinking: *I've got to get out of here.* I ran to the restroom, coughing and choking on my own blood. My hands were covered. I thought, *This is it, I'm going to die.* Oh, the thoughts that were running through my mind. I tried to convince myself that there was nothing wrong. The doctor even said so; this must all be in my mind. I cleaned myself up and went back to class to take my test. This became "normal" to me. I knew down deep inside, even if no one else knew, not even the doctor, I was going to die. Finally, an answer to my prayer, this way no one would know about the abuse, and

God wouldn't have to punish me if I told someone. It was then that I truly knew in my heart that He didn't love me. The circumstances were ugly, there is no doubt about that.

I was eleven years old when God revealed himself to me again. It was at church camp, my grandmother had been asked to be a camp nurse. My aunt's church was sponsoring this event and since we were living with my grandmother, my sister and I were able to go. We had a wonderful time there. No stress, no worries, it seemed as if we were free, at least for a while.

The church services for the kids were awesome; they weren't like our services at home. I couldn't help but be amazed by how many kids went to the altar, and how they would raise their hands during praise and worship. Being raised a foot-washing Baptist this just wasn't done. As I remember this, I can see the inside of the chapel, I can hear the kids singing, and the presence of God is very real. He is calling me to a point of understanding, I feel peaceful. He is telling me that He loves me and that this was my time to tell everyone that I was a child of The King, but I couldn't. I shook off the feeling; I was angry, unsure, and very confused. I couldn't help thinking: *Why would God choose me? He doesn't love me. I'm not worth anything, it has to be a mistake*. When I left the chapel that night, a friend whom I had met there walked with me as we started back to our cabin. It was getting late as we stopped at a little picnic area and commented on how beautiful the lake was. You see, there was a huge lit-up cross in the middle of that lake mounted to a small island. The stars were out and the moon shone just right on the cross. As we sat staring, we were joined by one of the counselors, I'm pretty sure he was a youth pastor. He asked what we thought of the service, and with minimal conversation we told him it was good. He began to talk to us about accepting Jesus Christ as our Savior and again I said nothing. I was ashamed and scared. It's hard enough being a preteen without all the problems facing me at that time. It all seemed too big for me, and it didn't matter, I couldn't change what was happening in my life. The counselor asked if he could pray with us, and we agreed. My friend accepted Christ and she didn't hesitate to tell it. Myself, on the other hand, continued in silence. I felt guilty and ashamed, feelings I had become accustomed to.

Our attention once again was drawn to the lit-up cross in the middle of the lake, only now there seemed to be some sort of commotion. Someone was in a boat on the lake! As the kids gathered 'round to see, the counselors were frantically trying to contain the situation. I listened and watched all the commotion, not realizing that my own miracle was about to take place. When I looked at that cross, it wasn't other kids that I saw. The lights on the cross became brighter, and as I looked, it seemed like an automatic camera zooming in on an object. My heart began to race and tears filled my eyes. The cross was not alone; Christ was hanging on it! I saw the nails in His hands and feet, His bruised body, the blood running down His brow as the crown of thorns pierced His head. I stepped forward to take a closer look; He lifted His head and our eyes met. At that moment my life would change forever. He was telling me how much He loved me. I turned away not wanting to believe. I asked my friend, "Do you see that?" She said, "Yeah, and boy are those kids in trouble." I realized that she was not seeing what I was seeing. My heart was humbled and I ran to my grandmother's cabin and bolted through the door. She sat staring at me, startled, and asked, "What is it?" I told her that Jesus had saved me, I had been born again, my heart was no longer my own, it belonged to Christ. Then it came, the shout I had come to know so well. She reached over, grabbed me and hugged me so tight, sobbing, shouting, and praising God for the victory. I had done it, I had admitted that God saved me, and I knew without a doubt, He had. Now I knew that He loved and cared about me, it wasn't hard to believe anymore. My heart felt peace and love that I had not felt since I was eight years old. Somewhere down deep I knew that He would make everything all right.

For that time I felt joy and freedom like I had never known. I didn't have a care in the world until it was time to go home. I remember my heart sank, I began to scream inside and the confusion returned. God wouldn't let anything happen to me now, would He? My joy was short-lived when the abuse continued and I began to wonder if my experiences with God were real. Had I been dreaming? Was it wishful thinking? I didn't understand. I didn't want to be wrong about God, but it seemed that the other shoe had just dropped. I began to question Him again, and my confusion was unbearable. It was becoming evident that He didn't love me. How could He do this to me, I felt like someone had played a terrible trick on me. How could He! I was being abused by someone I was supposed to trust with my life. I was very ill, and felt abandoned by those who were supposed to love me unconditionally. I couldn't imagine a loving God allowing all these things to happen. My life continued to fall apart within me. How would I survive?

I was raised in church, and I was taught that if you did this or didn't do that, God was going to get you. It doesn't take much to form a child's opinion in a negative or positive way. A few catch phrases or sentences at a very formidable time in their life will do it. If you take hell-fire and brimstone teaching, join it with a feeling of abandonment by divorced parents, sexual abuse, and physical illness, you've got a recipe for a child with insecurity problems, a child with feelings of being nothing and knowing they are not worth having any good thing. They set out on their life's journey, trying to please anyone and everyone. They are trying desperately to fit in or be loved. This result that they search for never comes through human form. Eventually, through every relationship and circumstance, those feelings will rear their ugly heads. I struggled for years, thinking if I did this or that, others would love me, but you know what? It didn't work. I just fell deeper into sin and strife, constantly searching for what I thought I needed. That same spirit of wanting to please became a path of self-destruction, not to mention it also allowed me to push people away even when I didn't mean to. It was hard for me to trust anyone. It was utter confusion. With all that was happening, it seemed that God didn't have a chance. Fortunately for me, I learned the more difficult the problem the greater God's victory. The greater the problem, the less chance that man will get the glory, and when there is no way but God's way, we cannot dispute the fact: God is in control and the glory belongs to Him. God was trying desperately to reach me, but not in the way that I wanted or needed, so I felt. It would take years, many miracles, an abundance of trials, and finally good sound teaching that would confirm that ultimate feeling I had felt as an eight-year-old child. I can say now that the visions gave me a thirst to find Him, whether I wanted to believe that or not. The seed had been planted. Only time, God's time, would reveal this to me. He is not waiting in anticipation for me to mess up so He can "zap" me. Instead, He was shedding tears as He watched me make the wrong turn time after time after time trying to find "my own way." The most amazing miracle of all is He never left; He was there all the time.

When things would get really bad, I would think of times that were so special to me, like walking the hills at my grandparents' or aunt and uncle's farm singing at the top of my lungs, I loved to sing. Those were peaceful times and I truly believe that those times are some of what gave me the strength to go on. God put two very special people in my life to show me what unconditional love is: an aunt and uncle. They loved me and I knew it. When I stayed with them on weekends or in the summer, I didn't have to worry about anything except being a kid. My uncle would teach me how to sing, play piano, drive a tractor, work on cars, and run a dairy farm. He is an awesome man. Some of my favorite times were when he would take me fishing; I believe he loved me like a father should.

My aunt taught me important things about life, like being gentle to a newborn animal, and how to take care of it. That it's okay to cry when things hurt you. She taught me how to laugh, and boy did we laugh a lot. The most important thing she taught me is how to love someone else. She loves me unconditionally, and is a wonderful woman to be respected and cherished. The love that they had shown me became crucial to my survival. However, the visions and glimpses of *you are someone, you matter, you are worthy of love,* that they had taught me, would become buried, unrecognizable by the life I would have to live when I was away from them. These things continued to get buried deeper as I hit the teenage years and felt the injustice of it all.

You know, Satan can't take light out of you—he can bury it,

but God will dig it up; it may take some time, but He will keep digging. You will begin to see a glimpse of light, and as it grows, the seeds of goodness planted so many years ago are no longer dormant. The "Son" shines and they begin to sprout, but the best part is yet to come. The roots will begin to take hold. They become strong and the next thing you see is a beautiful rose, genuine in character and beauty. You've finally found who you are in Christ, and He has set you free to love, live, and to be loved. My heart was never consumed with hate—hurt, yes—but not hate. It's kind of like searching for oysters in the ocean. You may have to pass through a lot of storms and do a lot of digging before you find that one precious pearl, but once you do, it keeps you digging for more. Why? It's worth it, it has high value, and it is priceless. Although there was a lot of pain in my life, there was also a lot of joy. Would I change it? If I did, then I would also have to give back all the joy that I have had. With all the wisdom and knowledge that comes with this life, I wouldn't change it. If I did my heart would not be in the right place for God to use me to help others. Therefore, I choose to make all those trials count for the glory of God. It's very simple once you can see what God is trying to do. He doesn't cause the bad things to happen, He gave us free will—freedom to choose our path. If we choose to live for Him, He will be there to turn the trials into something good and wonderful. That doesn't mean that we won't have to go through the fire, it simply means that He will be there to help us through. The awesome thing about this truth is that we become one step closer to being Christ-like. If we can stop for a minute, and see that God's victory is our victory, then a lot of the campfires wouldn't become forest fires.

My grandmother was a very influential part of my life; she has never stopped praying for me. She is an awesome prayer warrior, and she loves God with all of her heart. So many times I watched her pray and grieve over someone who was not saved. She is a diligent Christian woman who believes in the power of God.

I remember one time I had had a bad day at school, and when I came home she was working in her flowers, and she always had the most beautiful flowers. She asked what was wrong and I told her. She sat me on her lap in an old metal rocking chair outside in the yard. She wrapped her arms around me and told me that it would be okay. She prayed over me and then she told me how much God loved me. I wished she knew all that was happening in my heart and life at that time. I wanted to scream it out but, I couldn't, there was just too much at stake. If she knew, she wouldn't love me anymore. I couldn't risk it. For a child to carry a secret like that was hell in its purest form. I remember many nights lying in bed, praying in sobs for God to let me die. At such a young age this should not have been a topic for thought, but I felt as though that was my only escape. It would have been just fine with Satan had he succeeded, but God had a far greater plan.

A time after my parents' divorce, my mom announced that she was moving to California, and she gave us kids a choice to live with either her or my dad—we chose neither. My sister set the stage, she didn't want to leave her friends and my brother and I didn't want to leave our sister. There was so much strife in this situation, how could we choose my mom? This would mean, to them, that we didn't love our dad. How could we choose my dad, this would mean we didn't love our mom. What a predicament we were all in. I know my sister felt this was the only way to make a decision without hurting either parent. She was wise for being so young. In my opinion, children who are hurting this much should not be asked to make a choice like that. I'm sure this was assumed to be a decision in my dad's favor. What we really wanted was for the nightmare to end. Soon after my mom left, my dad became a truck driver and preached on weekends. This was a relief during the weeks he was gone, but the weekends were a nightmare. I would try and spend as many weekends and as much of the summer as possible with my aunt and uncle. There were times when I would sneak into the back of my grandparents' truck when my grandmother would go to work when we would arrive. I would call my aunt to come and get me. Unfortunately I wasn't very successful most of the time. We would get to the gate of the property and my grandmother would have found me and told me to go back to the house. As time went on, my dad wouldn't let me go as much anymore. My grandmother knew nothing of the abuse when she took us in or after as far as I know.

Even though my grandmother loved us and never said anything to us, I always felt we were a burden. My grandmother had to go back to work at the nursing home to help support us. My grandfather managed the farm and helped to look after us while she was at work. Make no mistake, it was hard and a lot of times we were left to take care of ourselves.

As I became increasingly ill my grandmother took me to a doctor. There was an exam and x-rays, but the reason for the illness was simple. I was suffering from a nervous disorder brought on by my parents' divorce, so the doctor said. As for the coughing up blood, I was sent home with a bottle of cough syrup. Life went on, high fevers and coughing up blood became normal to me. My grandmother, in an attempt to help me, would give me shots of an antibiotic and place a hot water bottle on my side, as it used to swell and hurt. The next morning I would be up and ready for school like nothing ever happened. I didn't complain much and I didn't talk about it. It was just simply supposed to go away.

One thing after another, life seemed to have no sympathy for the innocent. As time passed, we would see my mom less and less, about once or twice a year, as she lived out of state. However, I remember all too well this one incident. My mom had come for a visit with ulterior motives. The manner in which she did this left my sister and me devastated, as we didn't know she was coming until she was already here. My dad was on the road at the time, and my grandmother was at work. My grandfather was very apprehensive but agreed to let us go to dinner with her. She took us to her sister's house and told us that she planned to take our brother back to California with her; she asked if my sister and I wanted to come, too. My sister was crying incurably. I think she felt responsible for what was happening, as she had tried to become our protector and caregiver. I am sure my sister understood more than I did at that time. My mom gave my brother something that made him sleep and they returned to California. My aunt returned my sister and me to my grandparents' house. I remember crying a lot, and how angry my sister was. When we returned it was like nothing I had ever experienced. My sister called my grandmother at work; the wailing and the tears were unbearable. We were grilled for every detail. They contacted my dad and I thought, for sure, he would die of a broken heart. For months the tears went on and on, the yelling, the arguing on the phone between my parents was more than I could take. They hated each other and it was obvious to all concerned. We were told on more than one occasion how terrible my mother was, and this halted any notion, at that time, I had had to go and live with her, but the older I got, the more I would entertain the idea.

My brother was my dad's pride and joy and I could see that this pain cut deep. I had never seen my dad hurt like that before. I found myself having sympathy for him. I knew how much I loved my brother and how badly I was hurting; surely his pain was as genuine as mine. I retreated within myself, thinking we must have done something very bad to have all this pain. My brother, sister and I were very close when we were young. I think we felt that each other were all we truly had. This was very traumatic and shook me to my very core. Looking back, I know this was for the best, as we didn't have a lot of money and often times went without adequate clothing for winter, as well as other things. Because my grandmother had to work the swing shift, we often had to "fend" for ourselves. At least now, my brother would have a full-time parent and would have everything he needed.

When I was fourteen, my dad remarried. I really thought that the abuse would stop now—boy, was I wrong. The abuse increased and I knew that if I didn't get out of there my life would become even more devastating. I tried to gain the courage to tell him that I wanted to live with my mom, but I was afraid. I didn't know what he would do to me.

One night he came into my room and told me to get up and follow him. Reluctantly I obeyed. He took me to an old broken down van that he had parked in the yard. As I got into the back, I just remember thinking, *I can't fight anymore.* He instructed me to take off my clothes. I did, but this time something was different. I had decided not to fight. As I took off my clothes, I lay down, stretched out my arms and legs and said, "Okay, do what you want." He just looked at me in shock, and disgust. I'll never forget the look on his face as he stared at my fifteen-year-old, seventy-five pound body, and told me to get dressed. I was shocked! The game was over! I had lost the will to fight him off and at the same time he lost control over me. He lost the power to control me simply because I refused to fight. What a sick person. Had I known this, I would have given up a long time ago! The feeling in my stomach was one of horror and disgust at how disturbed this person was.

As I got dressed, he turned his back to me and I thought, *This is it, it's now or never.* I began to speak. I don't think I really cared what would happen anymore. I just knew that there had to be a better way to live. I told him I wanted to live with my mom, and as I held my breath, I was shocked at his response. With no hesitation at all, he said, "Okay." After I got dressed and went back to my room, needless to say, I didn't sleep very well. I just kept remembering all that he had done to not only me, but my sister as well—the time he tried to get us drunk so he could have his way. We were just kids. There were so many disgusting moments, although, there is one incident that is so ingrained in my mind that even to this day it frightens me.

One night, he came into the room my sister and I shared—we slept on bunk beds, hers was on top. I heard him come in, he looked at me to make sure I was asleep and then he climbed on the top bunk with my sister. It broke my heart as I heard her cry, begging him to stop, but he wouldn't. She kept crying and he slapped her. My heart was beating so fast I thought it would burst as I jumped out of my bed and screamed at him to leave her alone. His reply? "If you don't get back in that bed, you are going to get the same." As I crawled in my bed, I tried so hard to block out my sister's sobs for help, I felt so helpless. I was so afraid of this man! Why was this happening?! Why wouldn't God help us?! As I think of all this man has done to my sister and I, as well as many, many other victims, it sickens me to think this man is part of my DNA. I have forgiven him, yes, but forgetting is quite another story.

When I was nineteen years old, my stepmother had come to me and said she needed to talk with me. Her demeanor was very serious. As she began to ask me questions about my dad, I asked why she was questioning me. Her reply sent me into shock. She said that there were some "things" that he was doing to my stepsister, and that she needed to know if he had done the same to me. I loved my stepsister, she was the little sister that I always wanted, and to hear that he was putting her through the same hell that he had put me and my sister through was just too much to bear. I decided to tell the family of the abuse, thinking that they would be supportive and stop him. Boy was I wrong. They said that I was lying and, basically, some told me that God was going to get me for this. My sister wasn't ready to support me either. In an instant, I felt as though I lost my whole family, and time would confirm this. I gained the same reaction from my mother when I told her.

After eighteen years, my sister and I began to talk about the abuse. We had never "talked" about it before other than the first time I told the family, and even then it was very brief. I feel like the abuse that she endured was far greater than mine due to what she revealed to me. Just one incident that she told me sent my mind hurling. Just when I thought that nothing else this man did would shock me, it did.

My sister began dating when she was quite young. I am sure she was looking for someone who really cared about her and would make her feel special, and maybe even rescue her from this mess. When she was fifteen, she became pregnant by her boyfriend. Little did she know that her life would become even more devastating as my dad would rape her to try and "get rid" of the baby. After all, he was a minister of the gospel and this would embarrass him. She was basically forced to marry as well. As I think back, it is truly a miracle that we both survived.

I have been at peace with this part of my life for many years with the help of God and much counseling. However, as I write and I relive this, I have to say, it is not easy. My heart grieves for those who have endured such pain. I pray that my testimony will help someone else to realize there is hope and restoration.

My mom sent me a plane ticket and I was off, or so I thought. Neither my dad nor the rest of my family wanted me to go and thus I had to find my own way to the airport, which was over an hour away. Getting to the airport was a nightmare. I searched frantically to find someone to take me, and finally a friend of the family came through. Needless to say, I almost missed my plane.

When I sat down in my seat, I felt unbelievable relief and excitement. I knew that the abusive part of my life was behind me and now I could start fresh. I kept thinking about how I would be able to sleep through the night without fear. How I wouldn't have to worry about when he was coming home. I wouldn't have to worry about getting pregnant with my father's child. The excitement I felt on that plane was almost uncontainable.

I arrived in California, September 1981, and it didn't take long for the health problems I was facing back home to surface. My mom seemed happy that I had come, although, due to the history of our family, things were a little awkward, at least for me. I had many questions. Yes, she asked me to come live with her, but was it just to get back at my dad? We were told lots of things about my mom that were not good. Although, the picture that was painted of her didn't quite fit as I saw her at the airport, she did claim victory when I got off the plane. It was going to take time; this was the only thing I knew for sure.

It had been about two weeks since my arrival when my mom asked me to walk down to the corner store to buy her some cigarettes. I hopped on my bike, ready to go, and about half way there I started to get short of breath; I began coughing and left a trail of blood back home. I came in and sat at the foot of the stairs to rest. My mom came and asked if I had gotten her cigarettes, and when I said no, she asked why? Very casually I told her what had happened. My mom, being a nurse, became concerned. She thought that because I had a chronic cough, that maybe my throat was sore and that's where the blood was coming from, but she didn't know how much blood there was. She said, "Come down to my bathroom and show me." I followed her to the bathroom. I started to cough; the blood came and would not stop. My mom screamed for her boyfriend, who would later become my stepfather, but before he got there she fainted. He picked her up and put her on the bed. He asked what happened as we were trying to get her to come back. When she came to, she began to cry. I just looked at her and told her, "Mom, it's okay, it'll go away." She just cried harder. She picked up the phone and immediately called a doctor. He told her I needed to be seen right away. The next few weeks would consist of endless tests, doctor visits, many meetings with specialists, and devastating decisions.

The doctor, who became my consulting physician, was in my hospital room when the original x-rays from back home came. He held them up to the light and started to yell in his native tongue. He was from India, I think. I'm sure his words were not of great respect for the doctor who originally ordered the x-rays. I began to cry out of fear; he was yelling and pacing back and forth. When my mother addressed him, he said that if they had done something then, which was about one and a half to two years earlier, this wouldn't be happening to me now. After reviewing the x-rays in detail, he concluded that I had had pneumonia at least nine times. He said there were many scars, but nine were the ones that they could conclusively count. I was never treated for pneumonia up to that point.

Upon completion of many blood tests, x-rays, a bronchogram, and a bronchoscopy, in which they extracted a quart of pus and a pint of blood, they determined that the left lung could not be saved. Now came the hardest decision. What to do? Leave it and treat it? No, I wouldn't have a chance of survival. They had already determined that if I had not come to live with my mom, it was a medical certainty that I would have died in one year or less. I was fifteen years old and weighed seventy-five pounds. Should they remove the whole thing? This seemed to be the best way, or they could resection the lung, leave a portion in, which could help me or not. My poor mom, after having children of my own, I know the agonizing pain she struggled with making her decision. This was not the only pain she would have to deal with. She had to inform the rest of the family. I can still hear her cry from the painful words that were said. I didn't understand what was going on until I talked to them myself. They told me I wasn't really sick and that my mom was doing this just to get back at my dad. If this was so, then that would make my mom a monster, and this she wasn't. My mom had her own demons from the past to deal with, compiled with this; I can only imagine how she felt and the things she was thinking.

This devastated me, I knew all I had gone through in recent weeks, and I couldn't imagine it being a lie. I fell into depression and thus the surgery was postponed until my frame of mind was in a healthier state. At this point I just wanted to die, then I wouldn't have to listen to all the arguing and fighting, I could just be dead.

The doctor reiterated to my mom how dangerous it would be to go through with the surgery at this time. I was referred to the hospital psychiatrist to improve my state of mind. I don't really remember much about our conversations, except her telling me that my mom loved me and that she would never do anything like this just to get back at my dad. I do remember feeling numb and thinking that all these people cared about was hurting or getting back at each other. I felt extremely alone. *Where was God?* I wanted to scream out, "What about me?! Does anyone care about me?!" If only someone would hear me. I was angry. How dare them think of themselves at a time like this? If I died they would sit around blaming each other. Would anyone have stopped and cared about what I had gone through? Probably not! Would the madness ever end?

I was released from the hospital, as the surgery was scheduled for a later date. What I didn't know, at the time, was they didn't expect me to live anyway. The doctors told my mom that even if I made it through the operation, there was no guarantee that I would live past the next year. She made a wise decision in keeping this from me until months later when the whole ordeal was over. Had she told me, I'm sure I wouldn't be here today, as I think I would have willed myself to death.

It was now November and the holidays were rapidly approaching. Because the doctors were not sure I would make it, my mom decided on a date after my sixteenth birthday. I'll never forget the celebration we had, she made it very special. We also celebrated Thanksgiving at the same time, because the two dates were so close together. My mom is an awesome cook and she made a great meal. We celebrated as best we could, considering the circumstances. Everyone tried very hard to make it a special occasion, but the feeling in the house was one of sadness, fear, and uncertainty. I knew something was wrong and I was reasonably sure I knew why. However, it was one of those things you don't really talk about. I think everyone was just trying to get through the day. You know, we celebrate life when we celebrate a birthday. This was awkward to say the least. I can only imagine what my mom was thinking and feeling. How she got through that day without bursting into tears in front of me is something I'll never know.

If you can imagine from a parent's perspective, having a child come and live with you after four years of being separated, it's a little awkward. This child is in their teenage years and you don't really know who they are. Now this child is faced with a life-threatening illness that you have to help them through, and you haven't even had a chance to get reacquainted before you are thrown into the fire. Talk about your parental stress!

Now imagine this scenario from the child's perspective. You don't know this parent. The lifestyle you were raised in is completely opposite of what this parent lives. You were raised in church, fearing God through hell-fire and brimstone, and now you're living with someone who doesn't go to church, living with someone they are not married to, and they drink every night. You were taught that these kinds of people were very bad and hell bound. Now you are sick, away from the only home you've ever known, and living with a parent whom you don't really know. We are talking about mass confusion. HELP!

The day came for me to have the operation. I remember

feeling very afraid, but somewhere deep within me was the will to live, and I didn't know why. As they prepared me for surgery, I watched my mom very carefully. She was strong in her outer appearance, but I could see in her eyes how distraught and worried she was. We had a painful history and now we would have a long, painful road ahead.

The doctors had decided to take out the left lower lobe and treat the disease in hopes that it would give me a better chance in the future. They were not sure if it would help me or hurt me; only time would give the answer. They also told us that I probably wouldn't be able to use or move my left arm very much for about a year, due to them cutting the muscle under my arm. There would be physical therapy and doctor appointments every week, medication and x-rays for at least a year. The worst for me was the isolation, having a home tutor, and not going to school or making friends. Typical teenage thoughts, I was supposed to be social. This wasn't a very attractive future for a sixteen-year-old.

The time had come and the nurse gave me a sedative to calm me down. My mom kissed me and said she would see me in a little while. I remember watching her cry as she buried her face into my stepfather's chest as they took me away. It felt like a scene from an old movie. The only exception? This was real.

The operation should have taken about three hours to perform, instead it took five. I was told later that they had lost me on the table. The two extra hours must have seemed like an eternity without any certainty in sight. The longer the wait the more negative the outcome.

Finally, the operation was over, I had made it. When they brought me to the intensive care unit, I was moving my left arm up and down. I vaguely remember them telling my mom how amazed they were that I could move my arm. However, I needed to stop or I might rip out the stitches. I was obviously feeling no pain. The doctors and nurses were amazed at how quickly I was recovering. Because of this, they moved me to a regular room sooner than expected. The victory would be short-lived, as my life would literally hang in the balance.

I awoke one morning not feeling quite as good as I had been. The nurses did their routine check and I appeared to be fine. A short time later, I would take a rapid turn for the worst. It was becoming very difficult for me to breathe as I was drifting off to sleep. I felt as if I were floating, kind of like a dream. I could see myself lying in the bed, sleeping, as I drifted above the bed and moved to the corner of the room. I watched as the nurse came in to check on me. She ran out of the room and the next thing I saw were nurses all around me, and someone was holding down my feet. The doctor came in hurriedly, asking the nurses all kinds of questions. He took a tube and placed it in my nose. As they worked on me, I don't remember feeling any pain, as I continued to watch from the corner of the room. When the doctor was almost finished, I couldn't see myself anymore. I just felt this excruciating pain in my chest and I started to cough and cry. The doctor said, "She's back!" Later I was told that my lung was filling up with fluid; essentially, I was drowning myself. I had gone into respiratory arrest. The chest tubes were supposed to drain off the excess fluid, but for some reason, they weren't working. My mom had come in a short time later, devastated at the news, but relieved that I was okay.

Twice, I was on the brink of death, and twice, God spared my life. I was so "out of it" and distraught that I didn't see what God had done, nor did I care. I was just trying to get through all of this pain that was coming at me from every direction.

It is amazing what you will say or do when you are under the influence of drugs. My sub-conscience revealed itself in a "not-so-nice" way. Apparently, I told my mom how I felt about her leaving, and about all that she had done to my sister, brother, and me. Basically it was all her fault. Everything that had happened to me, I blamed her. It was inevitable that the pain would surface in this manner. My mom, later, told me what I had said. I don't remember saying those things to her, but knowing that I hurt her like that made me feel guilty for a very long time. It was something that my mom would not soon forget. I had brought up things that she had tried to bury within herself. Now, any guilt or pain that she had been feeling about the past became a reality. Many times I have wished that I had the knowledge and wisdom then that I have now. It would have been nice to sit down and talk with my mom about these things when I was well, but I just didn't have the confidence to do that. I was afraid of rejection, afraid that the reason she left might have been me.

The things I said to my mom would be forever embedded in her mind and for many years in her heart. She already felt guilty for everything that had happened and this just threw her into despair. To me it didn't matter, she had her pain to deal with and I had mine. It didn't seem that we were going to come together and resolve these issues any time soon.

I was finally able to leave the hospital, strict instructions followed. The head of my bed had to be elevated so I could breathe properly. Medication and breathing treatments were a must. Because I favored my left side during the surgery, I didn't stand straight up. Physical therapy would become a weekly routine to help me walk straight, and to strengthen my left arm. There would be doctor appointments and x-rays every Monday for about a year. A home tutor would help me complete my freshman year.

My mom took good care of me in every way except emotionally—this is where we always clashed. She worried when I came home from the hospital. There were times I would wake in the middle of the night to find her sitting on the foot of my bed making sure I was breathing. I can imagine her fear, knowing the uncertainty of the next year of my life.

As time went on, I became stronger and stronger. I started to venture out and make friends, as I was allowed to return to school in the fall. It seemed the stronger I got the more my mom forgot the ordeal we had just conquered. I began to fit into the routine of our family, and it seemed that things were coming along. However, I was very uncomfortable when evening came. My mom and stepfather would drink every night before dinner. When she drank, she would start conversations about the past. The nights became very long; she would start out saying some terrible things about my dad, which I agreed with in my heart, but I wouldn't dare reveal to her. She would then move through the rest of the family. If I tried to defend any member of the family, the table would turn onto me. She had told me that I wasn't my dad's daughter, that I had a different father. Time after time she would make me feel like the divorce was my fault, or that I had messed up her life. I had never felt comfortable with my mom even when she and my dad were together. As my mom would reveal things in her drunken state, it would tear my heart out over and over again. The drinking was severing any chance of a true relationship between us. The verbal abuse was becoming unbearable. One of the things she told me is that I wasn't a planned pregnancy, but a mistake. I would find out later in my life that my dad had gotten a thirteen-year-old girl pregnant and when my mom told him she was leaving him, he raped her. Imagine the shock when she went back to the doctor for her follow-up appointment, after having my sister, only to find out that she was pregnant with me. My sister and I are eleven months apart and my mom was only seventeen at that time. I tried to get her to understand that it wasn't my fault that she became pregnant with me. I didn't ask to be born, and at this point, I was wishing that I hadn't. This went on and on and on. There were times I just wanted to run, but to where? I knew I had to stick it out until I was eighteen. Then, and only then would I be free from everyone. I had a little less than a year to go, I could make it. I knew what I had to do; I would keep myself occupied with things outside of home. I would turn myself off to what was happening and just wait, I was getting good at this. I had managed to turn my heart off section by section, and was becoming increasingly successful at building this bomb inside of myself. I would choose when it would go off—no one else, just me, it was mine.

My mom was a very quiet and proper person when she wasn't drinking. However, I didn't know what to expect from her and so I just tried to stay to myself. When she would drink she was a different person. Even when she wasn't drinking, I was afraid of her, I couldn't talk to her. We didn't have "mother-daughter" conversations, although this is something I craved. She didn't know me; she didn't know my dreams, my hopes, my fears, and certainly not my deepest, darkest secret. There was no way I could tell her, she would destroy me with her words and rejection. I couldn't trust her with the bomb that was ticking inside me, but if she only knew that she had the power to snuff it out. Oh, we were quite a pair.

What I would learn about my mom is that she had been forced to create her own bomb. My mom never talked about her past much, unless she was drinking. This is how I found out that she had had a very painful and abusive childhood, in a lot of ways just like mine. I didn't realize, at the time, that she was reaching out, overcome with guilt and pain. The divorce was extremely painful for my mom, as she didn't really have a support system to get her through. She took a lot of this out on me. I was there, a constant reminder of my dad and all of the things he did to her, and the things he put her through. She was angry that us kids didn't come and live with her when she first left. She took that as we didn't love or care about her, and that she had failed. Me being the teen got fed up with it all. I would argue back and try to defend my family. It got ugly. Our nights consisted of arguing, yelling and crying, lots of crying. I would try not to say anything and go to my room, but that didn't work either. I was completely convinced that she hated me.

Looking back on things, we can always say I wished I would have done this or that, but the fact is, we wouldn't be who we are had we changed the past. The bottom line? God has a plan for us. If only we could see this early in our trial, I am sure that we would be able to deter a lot of our anxieties and fears. By going through trials, God brings us to a point of purity, if you will. Think of it like this: In order to make a beautiful gold wedding band, the gold has to go through extreme heat to be purified. When the gold is exposed to the heat, dross, or the impurities of the gold, are brought to the surface. It is then wiped away to reveal the beauty of the "pure" gold. This is what God does for us. We are the gold, trials are the dross. If we listen to God, He will bring us through the fire and wipe away the dross, thus exposing genuine beauty. Here is the catch: God gave us free will, and it is up to us to choose His path.

What I know now is that my mother was hurting and she was just trying to get through her own pain. There would be years of arguing, nasty messages on my answering machine, and long periods of not speaking to each other before I would come to truly understand my mother.

As life went on, I began to meet new friends. I met a guy who was seven years older than me, and with my mom's approval we began to date. He became a lifesaver, and would smooth over what my mom was doing; he made me feel like I mattered. We would talk for hours, and he was interested in who I was. He would rescue me from some of those horrible nights and take me out. He was giving me the love that I had been craving for so long. I fell hard for him.

A typical situation that happens daily in many people's lives is, when you feel no one loves you, and someone comes along that is willing to listen and shows you genuine affection, you fall for them. This was a very vulnerable time in my life and I felt like I was on top of the world when I was with him. However, reality would set in, as I would have to return home. The feeling in my stomach is hard to describe. I felt scared, not knowing what to expect—helpless, knowing that when I walked in the door, no one could help or protect me. Verbal abuse hurts as bad as physical abuse. No one can prepare you for how deep words cut into your heart, or how indelible they are written in your mind. The Bible tells us this in Proverbs. There is life and death in the power of the tongue. How many lives would be saved if we spoke in love instead of anger?

As our relationship grew, my mom began to accuse me of having sex with him. She only accused me when she was drinking. My heart was breaking, because it wasn't true at that time. The more my mom and I argued, the more it pushed him and I together. It was only a matter of time before we went further in our relationship. We began to spend more and more time together until we were inseparable. The day came when we became intimate. It was a devastating experience for me. I began to have flashbacks of the abuse earlier in my life. I cried and became very confused. He asked questions and I opened my heart to him. I told him everything. He was the first person I ever told. What a relief, finally it was out, but this relief was short-lived due to the anger he felt for what had been done to me. Now I had to worry about him telling someone else this awful secret. He finally calmed down and assured me that he would say nothing. My secret was safe with him, or was it? I still felt terrified about anyone knowing.

I knew what we had done was wrong, but at this point I felt he was the only person who truly loved me. He was definitely the only one who knew all that was in my heart, and so I justified my actions. What I didn't realize is that things are not what they seem, and all things come with consequences.

As our relationship grew, my relationship with my mom continued to decline. Just when I thought my life was attaining some happiness, it happened, the consequence for my actions—I became pregnant. There was no way I could tell my mom, she would kill me; she had already threatened to put my boyfriend in jail for statutory rape if she found out that we were sleeping together. I was petrified. In the meantime, I told my boyfriend that I might be pregnant; he didn't take it very well. He was adamant about not wanting children. He had never expressed this to me before, and I was shocked at his response. I began to see a side of him that I couldn't believe. He didn't want to be tied down and this set a plan into motion that I didn't think I would live through.

When I had my lung operation, the doctors told me that I would never be able to have children due to the stress it would place on my body. They had told my mom and I that if I got pregnant, I would probably die. My dilemma was growing in fear. At that time I didn't know which was worse, death or my mother. I knew that I wouldn't be able to keep this from her for long because she was a nurse, obviously she would know. My boyfriend and I talked about it and decided that I would have an abortion. Because I was almost eighteen, we had planned for me to move out of my mom's house right after my birthday, which I had planned to do anyway. At that time I would be four months pregnant. I would have the abortion and life would go on as normal, right? Wrong, very wrong! When I told my mom that I would be moving out after my birthday, she was not happy. She wanted me to live with her until I graduated. I told her I would still finish school, but that I wanted to move out. The next thing she did sent me spinning. It wasn't long after our conversation that she sat me down and said, "If you are planning to move out when you're eighteen, then I'm going to send you back to your dad now." I was in shock, stunned, and scared. You name it, I felt it, as she laid down a one-way plane ticket in front of me. I just kept thinking, *What am I going to do?* I began to cry and told her I didn't want to go back. She said fine, as long as I abided by her rules and lived in her house until I graduated. I agreed. The control of my life was not my own. It belonged to my dad, my mom, and my boyfriend. What was I going to do?

I maintained a low profile at home and talked to my boyfriend, as we would devise another plan. We decided that a couple days after my birthday, I would leave as if I were going to school, but instead, I would head for Sacramento, California. Once I arrived there, my boyfriend's family would take me in and help me.

I began to pack my things little by little in the trunk of my car. On the appointed day, I packed the remainder of my things into a suitcase and placed them in my car. My mom was supposed to go to work that day, but for some reason she didn't. I was so afraid that she would catch me as I left. I stayed as calm as possible as I entered the house for the last time. It was now or never. I told my mom I would take my brother to school and she agreed. I wanted to explain to him what I was about to do and tell him good-bye. He was twelve now and understood more than I gave him credit for. When we got into the car, my heart was racing and I felt like I was going to pass out. He looked at me and then to the back seat where my suitcase was strategically placed and he said, "You're leaving, aren't you?" I said, "Yes." He was happy for me, he knew everything my mom and I had gone through. We talked all the way to school and when we arrived I gave him a letter for my mom, explaining why I was leaving. However, the letter didn't tell her I was pregnant. I gave my brother strict orders not to call her from school, and not to tell anyone about the letter except mom. I asked him to give it to her after school. We hugged and said I love you to each other. I watched as he entered the school and then I left.

My boyfriend had given me money to get to Sacramento along with a $250 check for an abortion. When I got on that freeway, I felt free! Free of everyone who had hurt me, including God. He didn't help me when I needed it and now I didn't need Him. I was in control of my life now. I would go to Sacramento, my boyfriend would join me there later and life would be good. Little did I know that I was running straight into a hell storm, and hell was just heating up!

Sacramento is about six hours from Los Angeles, so by the time I got to my boyfriend's parents' house, things were just heating up back at home. My mom eventually found me and called to threaten my boyfriend's mom and me. She said she would send the cops to bring me back; however, because I was eighteen, there was nothing they or she could do. Needless to say, after all the commotion died down it was time to get down to business. I told my boyfriend's family what had happened and that I was pregnant. I also told them of our plans for an abortion. His family was against abortion and thus tried to talk me out of it. I never felt like I wanted to have an abortion. I knew inside that it was wrong and I didn't want to do it, but if I didn't, I would lose my boyfriend. What I didn't know is that I had already lost him. He had been seeing a good friend of mine even before I left Los Angeles. We were having some problems because of the pregnancy. I didn't realize that his reason for sending me to Sacramento was to take care of "the problem" and then leave me. It wasn't until months later that I found this out.

My boyfriend's sister and I started making necessary appointments for the abortion. I was almost five months along now. His mom and family were persistent about convincing me not to go through with this. They offered to help me in any way they could. I told them he would be angry and leave me. They stuck to their guns and said they would still help; after all, the baby was their family member, too. I began to think about what they were saying more and more. The fact that my boyfriend wasn't there made it easier to listen. They even offered to adopt the baby if I still felt this way after it was born.

The day came for my final appointment before the procedure. I was nervous and apprehensive to say the least. This was the appointment that would explain exactly what was going to happen. As the counselor talked with me, I remember thinking, *This is not happening, why should I have to make this decision?* As I read the literature and watched the video, I was so shocked. My heart grieved at what I was contemplating. I became more confused with my life, and was trying desperately to make some sense of it. How could I kill this baby? I could feel it move, it was alive! Was my freedom of choice more important than this life that could not defend itself or be heard? I left the clinic with a definite decision; less than twenty-four hours away from an abortion, I knew what I had to do. *I* had to defend this baby, *I* had to speak for this baby, and *I* had to change my mind. This was the right thing to do. If my boyfriend wanted to leave, then that was fine, but I was not going to kill another human being. When he would call that night, I would have something special to tell him.

I really felt he would respect my decision, but he didn't. He was very angry and it caused division with his family. He said things that hurt me so deeply, I just kept thinking, *It's starting again, only this time I have lost the one person that I thought truly loved me.*

As time passed, he would become even angrier. He had lost control of the situation. The time came when an abortion was no longer an option. I wanted this baby and I was going to fight. Now, reality set in, and I realized that I was carrying a life inside of me; it gave me hope. I would love this baby, it was mine and no one could take it away.

Time began to calm him down and we began to talk civil to

each other. He told me he loved me, but that he didn't want a child. I asked him to come to Sacramento so we could discuss our future, in hopes that when he saw me, all the bitterness would melt away. It was a fairy tale really. I thought that if he saw me, he would realize how much he loved me, and that we could get married and raise our baby. When I picked him up from the airport, we embraced and he told me he loved me. However, he told me that he couldn't stay and that he had booked a flight back to Los Angeles that night. In the meantime, we went back to his sister's house to talk. I remember thinking how good it was to see him. As we entered the living room, he sat on one couch and I sat on the other, we were facing each other. We talked for a while and then both of us just kind of gazed at the television, not really knowing what to say next. I looked over at him and he smiled at me very tenderly and I smiled back. He began to speak, and the words he said next shook me to my very core. As he smiled at me, he said, "I hope you know that I'm praying for this baby to die." I sat there in shock and disbelief. Needless to say, I went into hysteria. I got up, crying profusely, and headed for the kitchen counter to get my car keys. As I went for the door, he yelled at me to stop. When I didn't, he began to chase me. I got to the door and he pushed me down the stairs. I got up and tried frantically to get to my car as he grabbed me. I was trying so hard to get away but he was so strong. He pushed and pinned me with his body to the trunk of the car as he slammed my head down. I kept fighting, screaming and crying for someone to help me. His sister came to the door, screaming at him to stop. She told him that if he didn't stop she was calling the police. He grabbed my arm and dragged me into his sister's bedroom. He threw me on the bed and then jumped on my stomach. As he held my hands down, he just kept bouncing on my stomach, telling me that he was going to kill the baby one way or another. Someone began pounding on the bedroom door; his sister had called his best friend instead of the police. He was yelling through the door, threatening to break it down, and just as suddenly as the nightmare began, it ended. He stopped bouncing on me and let my hands go. He started apologizing over and over. He grabbed me and began hugging and kissing me frantically. I just sat there in shock, crying. I couldn't believe what had happened. He had never exhibited any violent behavior toward me before. He was always jealous and very controlling, but never violent.

When everything had settled down, he apologized again and told me how much he loved me and that we could make it work. I don't know if it was fear of him, fear of losing him or just plain stupidity, but by the time he got on that plane we were back together. He was moving to Sacramento and we were going to try and make it work, baby and all.

I think now, where was my brain? This was just an extension of abuse that I was already used to—sexual abuse, verbal abuse, and now physical abuse along with jealousy and control. I was just following the pattern that had been set for me as I was growing up. It obviously was affecting me in every aspect of my life.

He was my baby's father. I had to stay with him. I didn't have a choice, or so I thought. I was about six months along when this incident took place. It was a miracle that I didn't go into premature labor or lose the baby.

As time was moving forward I decided it was time to get myself into a routine and try to live normal. After the holidays, I registered at an independent study campus that had programs for pregnant teens. I knew I wanted to finish school and go to college; however, I didn't know how this was going to happen, but I had to take steps in that direction. Soon, my boyfriend returned to Sacramento and we tried to make it work. He had talked to his dad and decided that we would live in a travel trailer on his parents' property. I remember the trailer being very small, about eighteen feet. This is where we would live until the baby was born.

It wasn't long after his return that things began to take a wrong turn again. He became even more controlling and wouldn't let me come and go freely. He would check the odometer on my car to see how many miles I had driven and question me as to where I had been if there was even one extra mile on the car. There was one time he put a padlock on the outside of the door of the trailer so that I couldn't get out. He said he forgot I was in there. This was a camping trailer so it had no bathroom or shower. We took our showers in his parents' house; however, when you are eight or nine months pregnant, a bathroom is a precious commodity. He had left me in there for the day, until a family member came to find out what was going on and let me out. I became more and more afraid of him as time went on. A lot of the things he did were subtle, the kinds of things that people couldn't see or hear. I knew that if I defied him, there would be consequences. When we were around other people, all it would take would be a look from him to let me know that I was doing something that he disapproved of. Or, he would say something very subtle—no one else would know what it meant or what would happen later, but I did.

My life seemed to go from bad to worse; I should have turned to God, He was the only one who could have helped me. However, I had erased Him from my heart. I felt that He didn't help me when I needed it and now I didn't need Him. I was so far away from Him now that it would take a miracle to bring me back.

It was very hard to accept what was happening in my life. I was trapped and didn't know how to get out. The man who had shown so much love and compassion had changed. As I would learn through time and experience, he loved me as long as I did exactly what he wanted me to. Life was horrible. If I decided to do something on my own, or "think," that's when things would go from bad to worse. I just kept wondering, what was it going to be like when the baby arrived? Would he get better or not?

I was about to find out the answer to that very question. The time had come for the baby to be born, it was a very easy and short delivery. I remember checking into the hospital at ten minutes after five and delivering a beautiful blond-haired, blue-eyed baby boy at twenty-two minutes after six. It was at that moment I felt true love. As I looked into my son's eyes, I realized what it meant to be loved and also love. He was the most beautiful baby I had ever seen. I also felt ashamed, ashamed that I even considered ending his life through abortion. Satan used that very feeling to keep me in bondage for many years to come.

It wasn't long after the birth of this beautiful angel that my health would take a dreadful turn. When he was about four weeks old, I had a grand mal seizure. The seizure left me incoherent, I didn't even know I had a baby or what his name was for several days. When I finally came around, I was horrified that I couldn't remember. The doctors checked me completely and couldn't seem to find any answers as to why I had had the seizure. They referred me to a neurologist, and after many tests the conclusion was as strange as the seizure. They concluded that my body had been through enormous trauma and stress and therefore, it was trying to "escape." Needless to say, I became depressed as they put me on medication for the seizure, as well as reported the incident to the department of motor vehicles, whereby they revoked my driving privileges. Now I really felt trapped, even my body was against me.

The one comfort I had was my son. He was becoming more beautiful every day. He was the light of my life. For a time, it seemed that my boyfriend was coming around to the idea of fatherhood. We even had some very cherished moments.

I began to have more problems with my health as time went on. I decided to see an ear, nose, and throat (ENT) doctor along with a pulmonary specialist (lung doctor), because I was having trouble breathing. He determined that I had a sinus disease and decided on surgery for the treatment. He said that after clearing out the sinus cavity, I would be able to breathe better. However, when he got in there, he was shocked to find six tumors in the left sinus. He told me that normally when they find tumors like that, they are almost always malignant. I was stunned. I no longer wanted to die! I had something wonderful to live for, my son. What was I going to do? The doctor sent the tumors to be tested. He said he would let me know of the results as soon as possible. The thoughts running though my head went something like this: I felt in my heart that I was being punished for getting pregnant and having this baby out of wedlock, so I began to plead with God to let me live for my son's sake. What would happen to him if I died? Who would take care of him and love him like me? When the test results came back, I was relieved. The tumors were benign. No cancer here, I was so happy!

It didn't seem to matter what I did, I couldn't make my boyfriend happy. Life just kept going down this path. I knew I had made a lot of mistakes, I take responsibility for my part. I'm sure I did things to make him feel the way he did; however, abuse can never be justified. There was this one incident that completely crushed my heart. We had graduated from the camp trailer to a thirty-five-foot trailer and had moved it to a mobile home park. My son was a few months old at this point and I was growing weary of the situation. I told my boyfriend that I had had enough, and that I was leaving him. Before I could pick up my son, he grabbed him and slammed me into the door, knocking the breath out of me. As I slid down the door, almost passing out, he took my son to the back of the trailer. By this time the baby was crying hysterically. He was hungry and I needed to nurse him. My boyfriend wouldn't let me feed him. He made me listen to him scream for what seemed like an eternity. He told me that no one was going to leave him and that if I tried, he would take my son from me. I agreed not to leave and he finally gave me the baby. There is no greater fear than that of your child being hurt. I didn't know what to expect out of him at this point, so I agreed to whatever he wanted.

After this incident, it was even more evident to me that I needed to get out. I began to plan how I would leave him. This was not easy since I had no family to help me. This led me to a decision that was very difficult to make—I had to call my mom. The last time I had talked to her was the day my son was born. Before then, I had only talked to her one other time when I was about six months pregnant. I called to try and patch things up and to let her know I was pregnant. Needless to say the conversation ended very badly. When my son was born I called to let her know she had a grandson, and the conversation was very short. She asked if I was okay and if the baby was okay and when I said yes, she said good and hung up. That was the last time I had talked to her. This wasn't going to be easy.

My hands trembled as I dialed the phone and when she answered I almost hung up. I began to tell her what was going on and she said that I could come home. This was a big step for the both of us. As my plan took shape, so did the fear. When I look back now, I stand amazed at how God's hand was on me.

I packed my car for the trip, but rather than leave a note I decided to go to my boyfriend's place of business and tell him I was leaving. He worked at a convenience store, so there would be lots of people around. You are probably thinking that this is a not a smart thing to do. As it turned out, if I hadn't done it this way, he could have had me arrested for kidnapping—that's another story. I entered the front door of the store and went to the front counter to stand by the exit door. My heart still races when I think about this moment. After he was done helping a customer, I told him I was leaving him and then took off running as fast as I could for my car. He jumped the counter and chased me. I jumped in my car and locked the door. My window was down about an inch or so, and he grabbed the window, pounding frantically on it as I drove off. I was so full of fear that I thought my heart would explode. I headed for the freeway and didn't stop for anything except gas. When I reached my mom's house I knew I was safe from him. He would never think to look for me there, as he knew the relationship between my mom and me. Eventually he would find out where I had gone and call, and call, and call. Finally I gave in and talked to him. You would think that he wouldn't have cared that I left, but the fact that I left on my own without him telling me to get out of his life was more than he could take. He couldn't control me as long as I wasn't with him. It is hard to get out of a relationship like this. People like him control your mind; they make you feel and think that no one else will love you or want you. You are made to feel like you are not worth anything. It's hard to explain the control they have over you.

I talked with him and he told me how much he loved me and that he missed me. He made promises and convinced me that things would be different. I wanted to believe him and, I loved him. He was my baby's father! I gave in and went back.

My mom tried to convince me to stay and start college. She really did try and help. It seemed, for a time, that we were beginning a new relationship on a mother-to-mother level. She even stopped to see the baby and me on her way to a conference when my son was about seven months old.

Upon my return, he kept some of his promises, but it wasn't long until the control and verbal abuse began again. Now he was trying to find ways to prove me to be an unfit mother. If the house was not clean the way he wanted, he would become angry and verbally abusive, letting me know that a court would take my son away from me for that. I was only nineteen years old, I didn't know whether he was right or wrong, but I didn't want to take any chances. I became more and more frightened, not so much at the abuse, but that someone would take my son away. I loved my baby and I took very good care of him.

I remember an incident when my son was four months old. I had just gotten out of the shower and placed him in the middle of the bed. He rolled over and went chin first off the bed. I rushed him to the emergency room. The fall had bruised his chin, lip and gums. The emergency room doctor questioned me like I was a criminal. Fortunately, my son's pediatrician was on call and he came in to see him. He told the emergency room doctor that I was an excellent mother and that he had never seen anything that would indicate abuse. He also told that doctor that my son was well loved and cared for. That doctor apologized for what he had insinuated. However, my boyfriend tormented me for "letting" him fall off the bed. It seemed that everywhere I turned I was in fear for my son and myself. That was the only time he was hurt in my care.

As my son grew, he became curious as all children do. It was at this time that his father would go to far. My son was playing with the Rolodex by the phone. His father didn't like that and told him no. He continued to play with the Rolodex, and it was then that our lives would take a drastic turn. My boyfriend picked him up by one arm and tossed him across the living room, his head missing the corner of the room divider by inches. I gasped as I went to pick him up, he wasn't even walking yet. I was comforting him as his father was yelling at me to keep him away from the Rolodex. I knew that that was it. It was one thing to hurt me, but don't hurt my baby. I began yet again to plan another escape. This time, I called my grandmother from my hometown in Tennessee. She said she would send me a plane ticket so I could come and stay with her. By this time I think that my boyfriend had had enough, too. I talked to him and he agreed to let us go. This was a miracle! He knew when we got on that plane we were not coming back. Little did I know this would be his ultimate way of "getting back" at me. I held my breath right up to the time we got on the plane. My boyfriend and his sister took us to the airport and, as we boarded that plane, I began to feel new hope for a better life for my son and me.

Soon after our arrival my son and I began to settle into our new life. I got a job in management at a restaurant. My aunt and sister helped take care of my son while I was at work. It seemed that things were going to be okay. I began to date someone I had grown up with. He was a wonderful man and to this day I still feel that way. He treated my son as if he were his own. He had a very warm and compassionate heart. Just as it appeared that our lives were taking a wonderful turn toward happiness, it began to crumble. While at work one night a man came into the restaurant and asked for me. When I confirmed who I was, he served me with court papers to take my son away. I felt like someone had hit me in the stomach as I fell to my knees, sobbing. I couldn't believe what was happening. My ex-boyfriend was filing for custody of my son. He never wanted the baby. He tried to make me have an abortion, not to mention the abuse. How could this be happening?! I was nineteen years old at the time and didn't know much about the legal system. I talked to some friends and family members and they said you have to go back and fight this. Knowing what I had been through with this man, I didn't think there would be a problem. I talked with him on the phone a few times before I went back and his words to me were, "No one leaves me!" I had said to him, "You knew I was leaving you when you took us to the airport." The words that came next shocked me to say the least. He said that I didn't deserve to be happy, and, I quote, "Paybacks are a bitch." My life once again began to unravel. One of the biggest mistakes I made was giving my son his last name at birth. This gave him a legal right to fight. Being eighteen at that time, desperate to belong and confused, I was also ignorant, trying to live a fairy tale. By the time my son was born, I thought that things would work out, that we would marry, and live happily ever after. Obviously, this is not how it turned out. This was only the beginning of many more decisions that would lead to heartache.

In the midst of all of this, some of my family members had been talking to him and took his side, and others had told me I should get married tó my, then, boyfriend, as it would look better for the courts. It would deem more stable and more creditable than him. So, I did just that. I married before going back to fight custody for my son. What I didn't know was that my ex was painting a picture of me that was going to be very hard to fix. He was there, I wasn't, and I hadn't talked to anyone in the legal system yet. I was being portrayed as someone who was unfit to be a parent as well as having a psychological disorder. When I boarded the plane to go back to California, I had no idea what was about to happen to me, or my son. Little did I know that we were about to embark on a two-year custody battle that would end in a devastating tragedy.

Upon our arrival, the judge ordered us to go to family court services. There, they would determine who would get our son. His father accused me of kidnapping. I was completely blindsided and not prepared to fight this battle. He had a lawyer, I didn't, and obviously he had been preparing for this for quite a while. I had not prepared to fight to this extent. Why should I? He didn't want our son. This whole turn of events came about because he lost control over my life. Did he love my son? I truly did not think so.

When we went to family court services, I was emotional to say the least, but because of those emotions they felt his claim had validity. The result? The courts gave us joint legal and physical custody, six months of the year with him and six months of the year with me. I was devastated, I didn't live in this state anymore, what was I going to do? The court set the schedule and I had no say in it. My son would have to live with this schedule until he was ready to enter school, and then we would have to come back and do this again. My heart was crushed. Because I had had my son for the past several months, they gave him to his father first. If this wasn't bad enough, they gave my ex retro time of three months. This would mean I wouldn't see my son for about nine months. I just kept thinking, *How am I going to leave him with this man?* How would I explain to him that Mommy wasn't leaving him? How could I tell him that I didn't have a choice? Did I have a choice? Did I have to return? What would have happened if I had not returned, would things be different? There were so many questions. However, I had found out that if I had not returned to California for the court date, my ex had purchased a plane ticket to come and kidnap my son. He told me this himself and showed me the plane ticket. I felt I had no way out, this man would have control over me for the rest of my life, not to mention my son's. My hope was gone. I couldn't stay in California. I was married now, what was I going to do? If I stayed I wouldn't be able to see him, as it was not my turn. How was I going to leave my baby?!

My ex invited me to have dinner with my son and him the night before my flight left, to say good-bye. For my son, I agreed—bad decision. He would try and convince me to come back to him. It was a very emotional dinner to say the least. As the night went on, it would go from bad to worse. We were drinking alcohol with our dinner while discussing our son; he asked if I wanted to tuck him in one last time. Too many emotions and too much alcohol, one thing led to another and the next thing I know I am waking up the next morning beside him. He was pleased with himself and he didn't hesitate to tell me so. I boarded the plane and my heart literally felt like it was being ripped out of me. I felt as if I had messed up my whole life, and the life of my son. How could I do this to him? How could I betray him like this? Would he still love me? Would he ever be able to forgive me? I cried all the way home. The betrayal I felt was compounded as I got off the plane and saw my husband standing there. Such love in his eyes. He hugged me and said it would be okay. He said we would get a lawyer and fight this. If only he knew what I had done, he would hate me, too. It was just another secret to hold, just another hell. My life was eating me away and I didn't know how to stop it!

The one thing I could always feel without trying was guilt. It wouldn't take long for it to overcome me to the point of destruction. I soon started to feel like I didn't deserve to have my son because of what I had done to him and my husband. I didn't deserve to be happy or loved. This was my punishment and I had to live with it.

From the time I returned I couldn't be intimate with my

husband because of what I had done. He was patient with me, but soon began to question what was going on. I decided to try but I couldn't, the guilt overwhelmed me. I just knew if I told him what I'd done, he would leave me. I also knew that we could not continue this way, I had to make a decision. I decided it was time. I had to tell him. I sat up in bed and said, "I've got something to tell you." As he looked at me with those warm, compassionate eyes, I began to cry. I felt ashamed, how could I hurt him like this, how could I tell him? He didn't deserve this hell that I was dragging him through. I told him. He was angry, but he just held me and told me that he loved me and that we would get through this. I think that had the circumstances been different, it would not have gone like it did. However, the way he responded showed me that I could trust him with my feelings. As time went on, I would tell him of my "other" secret—he responded the same loving way and helped me through the difficult time that would follow. This would lead us to confront family members, but I knew I would get through it as long as he was by my side. I had never experienced love like this before, such understanding and compassion. My battle had become his. I couldn't believe his actions, it seemed like a dream. He truly loved me, and he forgave me. God had sent someone to rescue me. Did I recognize what He was doing? No! I was so grief stricken over my son that I could barely function. It took three months for me to say enough. I told my husband I had to go back and fight. I called my mom to ask if I could stay with her and she agreed. My uncle had planned to go with me; however, I didn't have money for a plane ticket, so he gave me his. The plan was that he was going to help me fight for my son, but it didn't work out that way. It seemed that no matter how good the plan or intentions, I always came up short.

When I arrived in California, I stayed with my mom. My

stepfather gave me a job with his company, and I kept in close contact with my husband. This distance would prove to be too much for us, and finally, we decided that he would come to California and stay until the custody issue was resolved.

I contacted my ex and he agreed to let us see my son on weekends. We would drive six hours every weekend to see him. The day-to-day caring for him seemed to change my ex to some degree. He appeared to be more caring. However, I wasn't about to trust this facade.

It was so good to see my son! He hadn't forgotten about his mommy, I was so relieved. The time spent with him was cherished. We were not allowed to take him anywhere, which made things a little awkward, but it didn't matter. I was just so glad to see him, to touch him and to take him in my arms and hug him. Leaving him was so hard, but I knew that it was just for a short time now. Up to this time, we had just visited my son and had not yet hired an attorney.

The going back and forth, finances, along with missing family began to take its toll on my husband. I was so preoccupied with getting my son back that I wasn't taking care of his needs, nor was I thinking of his feelings. This was something I would soon regret. He and I sat down, talked through the situation, and decided to divorce; we had been married almost a year at this point. I knew what I had to do, and I knew that he wasn't happy. It wasn't fair to drag him through my mess of a life, and so he returned to Tennessee and I stayed in California. He is a wonderful man; however, I felt I didn't have time to be the kind of wife he deserved or needed. This was better, now he could find someone worthy of his love, settle down, have kids, and be happy.

I continued to work for my stepfather and went to Sacramento every chance I got. My mom and I had been getting along okay, but she was still drinking and the trend from my teenage years would soon return. We began to argue and the arguments would last for hours. She would tell me how badly I was messing up my life. I didn't need her to tell me that, I already knew. There would be one argument that could not be fixed. I had been to see an attorney to discuss custody of my son. He said that I would need a $2500 retainer fee in order to start proceedings. I didn't have that kind of money and so I asked my mom if I could borrow it. Without hesitation, she said no. She had been drinking and we began to argue. She accused me of being an unfit mother and that she, herself, was going to go to court and take my son away from me. I had had all the stress I could take at that point. I yelled at her, she slapped me and the argument continued. I finally had had enough so I left. I didn't have anywhere to go and no money to get there. I ended up sleeping in my car just inside the gates of my stepfather's offices. I did this for several days until he came to work early and caught me washing my hair in the sink. He asked what I was doing. Humiliated, I told him. He took me to breakfast and gave me his credit card so that I could get a shower and a good night's sleep. My stepfather is a great man, he doesn't really say much unless he has to. I will never forget what he did for me that day. If it had not been for him, I don't know what would have happened to me. He made some phone calls, and made arrangements for me to stay with my stepsister.

The argument left me devastated. At this point I really didn't care about anything except my son. I had decided to move closer to him so I wouldn't have to drive back and forth. It was getting closer to the time when he was to come and stay with me. However, I would soon find out that his dad had a different plan, he was going to take me back to court and say that because my son had been living with him for the last nine months, that he shouldn't be uprooted from his "stable" environment. I had no doubt in my mind that the court would rule in his favor because my life had become very unstable in recent months. The only way I could stop this, or so I thought, was to get back together with him. For me, it was the only way I knew to be close to my son.

It was only a matter of time before my life would take on its familiar course. It had seemed that he had genuinely changed. However, this was short-lived when the verbal abuse and control over my life returned. I was becoming very depressed with no will to live. I just wanted to die at this point. While I was hitting bottom, my boyfriend was keeping records of my depression and my wrongs, as he had always done. I felt alone once again.

As I write and relive this, I can't believe all that I did, and all that I went through. Sure, I was unstable, but was it justifiable? I can't say; knowing what I know now, I believe we should take responsibility for our actions; we have the power to change our lives. How? I was trying to go in the right direction but I was getting knocked down at every turn. Why? The reason is simple: I was trying to be in control of my life, when I should have been letting God be in control. This is a good example of what can happen when we try to navigate our own destiny instead of letting God navigate. Will you let Him be in control of yours?

As time went on I was beginning to accept my life once again. It seemed as though I was destined for this kind of road and no matter how hard "I" tried to change it, this was my path. No matter how destructive, this is the one I was to walk down.

Life as normal? Yeah right! There is nothing normal about abuse. It would just get worse as time went on and I would finally say enough yet another time. The incident that changed our life was cruel and devastating to say the least. We were trying to potty train my son. I'd say he was almost two years old at this point, and he seemed to be having a difficult time of it, more than normal. I wasn't really concerned as he was still very young. However, his father was getting frustrated with him. My son had soiled his diaper early in the morning, he was still in diapers at night. His father stripped him down, in anger, put him in the shower and ran cold water over his little body. He kept telling him how bad he was for soiling his diaper and that if he continued, this is what would happen to him. My son screamed and cried for me. My heart felt like it would be ripped out of my chest as I stood there and watched in disbelief. I was horrified! My baby just stood there screaming and shivering. I was finally allowed to go to him and I wrapped him in a towel and held him until he calmed down. His dad went to work and I called the authorities. They suggested that my son and I go to a shelter for battered and abused women. This would set in motion a battle that nearly destroyed me, literally, but in the end, saved me.

We entered the shelter and they recorded the incident. They would help in any way they could, including legal help. We stayed there while I tried to get on my feet. One of the steps was getting a restraining order against my son's father. Another girl from the shelter and I went to file all the necessary paperwork. When we were done, my son and I were on the elevator going to the first floor. When the doors opened, imagine my shock as I stared right into the face of his father! Beside him stood a very well dressed man, his attorney! Needless to say I was terrified as I was pushing the buttons frantically trying to get the doors to close. As they did, I saw his attorney running up the stairs to get to us. When the doors opened, I ran the opposite way of the attorney. I ran back down the stairs, as there were stairs on each side of the elevator, and out of the courthouse. The Sheriff and his deputies were gathered just outside of those doors; I grabbed them, begging them to help me. Just as I said this, my ex and his attorney emerged. They explained their side and I explained mine. They also told the Sheriff that they were due in court to relinquish my parental rights and to bring kidnapping charges against me. The Sheriff just looked at me and said that he would escort me to see the judge, so I could tell my side. The judge gave me temporary sole custody until the next court date.

Let me stop here for a moment and just say that God not only had his hand on me in this situation, but He was slapping me with it! If I had not been in that courthouse on that day, at that time, my parental rights would have been relinquished and I would have ended up in jail or worse. That is how serious and detrimental my situation was, and I believe that would have thrown me over the edge, I have no doubt in my mind whatsoever. When I look back, it is amazing to see how God worked His miracles in the midst of this mess. I was so consumed with all that was happening to "me," that I failed to see His divine intervention until years later. This was definitely a crucial point in my life.

When I returned to the shelter, I told them what had

happened. They gave me instructions as to what to do next. I received counseling right away and this was wonderful for me in more ways than one. I had someone to talk to, someone to confide in. Now all I needed was an attorney and things just might start to look up. I called legal aide and they put me in touch with a wonderful attorney who took my case pro-bono, which meant I didn't have to pay him. This was a good thing since I didn't have any money to pay him. This man was wonderful. I know that God placed "this" attorney in my life.

At first, he was very hard-core business, but as he began to build my case, it was obvious, for the first time to someone other than me, that what was going on was very wrong. He fought for my son and me for two years. Finally, someone was on my side!

Things seemed to be turning around, slowly, but they were turning. We went back to court and the judge ordered all of us to get a psychological evaluation. In the meantime, he also ordered visitation for my son's father. My attorney advised me to do this. I continued in counseling as well as seeing the court-appointed psychiatrist. Upon completion of the evaluations, we returned to court only to have my son removed from my custody. The psychiatrist had written in his report that I had a passive-aggressive personality disorder and that I would run away with my son. Once again, my son was taken from me and I was only allowed supervised visitation with him. I felt like a criminal. My attorney assured me that everything would be okay. He said we would take this time and prove them wrong. We needed to prove I was stable and capable of taking care of my son. I stayed in counseling, got an apartment and a job. Things were looking up. I even started college.

During this time, my son started developing some health problems, such as trembling when he would try to put his blocks together. When he would walk his feet pointed outward, and if he fell down on his bottom, he would cry, turn blue, and faint. I would talk to his dad about this and his reaction was, "There's nothing wrong with my son." He wouldn't let me take him to the doctor, so I had to get a court order. The doctor said the tremors in his hands were from frustration in trying to put his blocks together, and that this was normal. As for the fainting, this was due to temper-tantrums, and his feet? They said he may need braces on his legs and referred him to an orthopedic doctor. Every problem had an answer.

I made an appointment with an orthopedic doctor. They took x-rays and examined my son. They said there was nothing wrong with his bones and asked if he were having any other problems. I told him yes and explained about the tremors, fainting spells, and the fact that he couldn't even run. He was almost two years old by this time. The doctor told me that my son needed to see a Neurologist, not an orthopedic doctor. I called his pediatrician to get a referral. By this time, his dad was angry and getting angrier by the day. He was adamant: "There's nothing wrong with my son!" It was a fight all the way. I knew something was wrong, I could feel it!

We soon returned to court and this time everything was in order. My counselor had written a report on my behalf. All my paperwork was in order and I had done everything the court had asked. However, my son's father had lied on his financial declaration and was coming after me for child support. We also found out that he had paid the psychiatrist to write that damaging report. The judge agreed that he and his attorney had been less than honest. He ordered joint legal and physical custody due to my son being ill, although we didn't know exactly what was wrong as of yet. He also ordered him to pay all my attorney fees. Things were definitely looking up.

It seemed as though life was just beginning now. The victory was mine. Now if we could get my son healthy, life would be good.

We were alternating times equally for visitation, as we were trying to "tolerate" each other. It was his visitation time when significant problems begin to arise. He still insisted that there was nothing wrong with "his" son. When I picked my son up to bring him home, he had stopped walking and had reverted back to crawling. I asked why didn't he call me? His comment was, "Because there is nothing wrong with him." I immediately called and made an appointment with the neurologist.

The words that I would hear that day would rip my heart out. As the doctor examined him, he found that my son had no reflexes whatsoever. In fifteen minutes the doctor concluded that my son had a degenerative disease. He wasn't sure what it was, but they were certain that he was going to die. They couldn't tell us the name of the disease without further testing, nor could they tell us how much time he had left. I sat there in shock as my son looked at me with those big blue eyes and smiled. His father just kept insisting that there was nothing wrong.

The doctor scheduled a nerve biopsy to pinpoint the disease and give it a name. There would be E.E.G.s, spinal taps, blood tests and many more tests before they would find out the name of the mystery disease. There would be physical therapy to keep his muscles from contracting to the point where he couldn't move. Months would go by and he would go from a normal two-year-old little boy to an infant-like state.

Finally, the news came, and a simple urine test was all we had ever needed. The test was conclusive: our son had a rare nerve disease called Early Infantile Metachromatic Leukodystrophy. He had a year or less to live. My heart was shattered and my mind was tired, so tired. Just when I thought my life would have some peace and happiness, now I would be forced to watch the most important person in my life die. In a single moment it seemed everything else in life was trivial compared to what my son was going through.

The holidays had arrived and just before Christmas this disease would take its hold on my son's life. It was my visitation time and I had made great plans. I had purchased items that he could play with sitting down. This was his Christmas and nothing was going to ruin it. Up to this point my son could still talk, use his arms, and he could still somewhat sit up, but he needed some help.

When I picked him up from his father's house, he had a little cough, nothing major. I didn't think very much of it. As the night went on, he would get worse. His fever shot up without warning. I called the doctor and he said to bring him in right away. They admitted him to the hospital and ran some tests. He had pneumonia. I asked the doctor how could this be? He wasn't sick earlier except for a cough. The doctor told me that the disease had progressed and was moving into advanced stages. This was the beginning of the end. They didn't expect him to live through the night. As they prepared to take him to the intensive care unit, I became angry. I started pushing furniture and throwing chairs. The nurses pulled me outside his room and informed me that if I didn't calm down, they would have to ask me to leave. I just looked at them through my tears and said, "You don't understand." They left me in the hallway to calm down. It was at that moment I began to call out to God.

I was hurt, devastated, angry, I felt like someone had just taken the life out of my body. My life was flashing before my eyes and I just kept asking, "Why?!" How could He do this to me! How could He take my baby away! As I leaned my head against the wall, sobbing, I heard someone call me by my first name, "Tammie." I said nothing, and again I heard someone call my name, "Tammie!" I turned to see a nurse standing there, and the words she said to me were so profound. She said, "You know, you can let this disease take advantage of you, or you can take advantage of this disease." I didn't know what she meant as I turned back to face the wall. When I regained my composure, I turned to talk to her, but she was gone. My son's room was at the end of the hall with no doors going out and nothing in the room across from him except and empty bed. When I asked the nurses in my son's room about the other nurse, they just looked at me blankly and then at each other and said, "We are the only ones working this floor tonight. I was puzzled, but the words she said kept ringing in my ears. What did she mean? How was I supposed to take advantage of this disease?

A few days had passed and, miraculously, my son was released from the hospital. He had made it. His father and I talked about what to do next. Because he was so ill, we had to discuss the fact that passing him back and forth wasn't good for him. We would argue about whom he would stay with. Due to our past, I would fight to keep him. However, his father was on disability from a back injury, which allowed him to stay at home. I was apprehensive to say the least, but someone had to give in for my son's sake. I don't think either one of us wanted to go back to court at this point. After consulting with the doctors, I made a decision that was both painful and fearful. The doctors had stated that because of the nature of this disease, my son would soon experience excruciating pain. They explained that his nerves were like an electrical cord, and if you plugged that electrical cord into an outlet, stripped the insulation from it, and then touched it, what would it do? It would shock you of course. This is what was happening to my son's nerves. The myelin sheath was being eaten away from his nerves, leaving them exposed. My heart was breaking just knowing what he was headed for, how cruel this disease is, and it would prove to show no mercy. After this explanation, I decided to give it a rest and let my son stay at his father's house; however, there would be many conditions. I would be allowed to spend as much time as possible with him, and I would be allowed to come anytime I wanted. His father agreed. I actually got to see him more with this arrangement than before.

Life became an array of doctor appointments, as well as around the clock care and a visiting nurse. We got along as long as the conversations didn't veer from my son, although some of those conversations were very heated. We would have to agree to disagree most of the time.

We both managed to begin new relationships in spite of this trial. The gentleman I had been seeing started out as a good friend. I brought him to meet my son before the illness took over his body completely. He could still speak a little. My son loved him right away. My friend was very soft spoken and gentle with him. He played with him every time he came to visit. I was truly amazed by this man. As time would pass, we would move in together as friends. His roommate had moved out and he needed a new one. I agreed. It wasn't long before the relationship grew into more than just a friendship. He is a wonderful man. He didn't just love me, he loved my son also, and he would prove to be very faithful as I traveled this road with my son and him. I asked him one time why he stayed with me. I was very involved and caught up in my son's illness. He didn't have to stay, he took a back seat to all of it. He told me that it was my son's turn to sit in the front seat and that soon enough, it would be his turn. This is one reason that made me fall into a very deep love with this man.

When my son became ill, I started to cry out to God. Most of my crying was blame, blaming God for my son dying. I couldn't understand how He could let this happen to an innocent child. If it was me He wanted to punish, why did He have to include my son? The answer was revealed to me when I had talked to a family member who was very close to my heart. They had said my son was dying because I had lied about what my dad had done to me. Would this ball and chain ever stop following me around? They said I had touched "a man of the cloth" and that this was God's way of punishing me. I could not get away from this and now I had dragged an innocent baby into this mess.

This just reiterated what my dad had said so many years ago; it would be my fault, and it was. Why did God hate me so much?

The arrangement we had made for my son lasted a few months before it became detrimental to his health. By now, he couldn't speak and could barely move. The pain was starting as well as other problems. He had to have a nasal gastric tube placed in his nose that went into his stomach so he could eat. His esophagus was damaged so he had to take medication to help keep his food down. Otherwise, he would just continue to vomit. He was losing weight drastically and I began to question this. The doctors said it was normal; however, they didn't realize how much weight he was losing. Then it happened, the day I had dreaded. I called to check on him. His dad was frantic and said he was having a seizure and probably was not going to make it, and then he hung up on me. I immediately called back and talked to the nurse and she said the same and then hung up on me. I called back again to tell them I was on my way over. This time someone I didn't know answered the phone and when I asked to speak with my son's father, he said, "They are not here." When I asked where were they, he said he was instructed not to tell me. Needless to say, I was in a panic and began calling my son's doctors.

After reaching his pulmonary specialist, I found out that he was on his way there. I asked the doctor not to see him until I arrived and he agreed. I must have driven ninety miles per hour through the middle of town. I arrived before they did. As I sat waiting, all kinds of thoughts kept running through my mind. When they entered the waiting room, I thought I would pass out. My son was bluish gray in color and he was seizing, his little body was bowed backward. As his father walked toward me, he dropped him in my lap. He then informed the doctor not to let me in the examining room as I was crying inconsolably. The doctor just simply said, "If she can't come back, then I can't see him." I could not believe what was happening. After the doctor examined him, he admitted him to the hospital. It was determined that he was suffering from malnutrition. The doctor asked if his medicine was being given to him. My ex replied, "As much as I can get down him." At this time, we all knew what that meant. He then went on to ask the doctor to stop feeding him or just give him a shot that would kill him, since he was going to die anyway. The doctor was in shock and replied that that was not an option. He was not going to kill my son by shot or starvation. The doctor set up a meeting with all of us after he had consulted with an attorney.

My fiancé and I, as well as my ex and his fiancée, met with the doctor for a progress report and discussion of where we go from here. I had requested that my son come and live with me from now on. His father wouldn't hear of it and continued to argue with the doctor about killing our son. The doctor reiterated the fact that he would not take that position in my son's health care. Angry that he had no control, he stood up and said, "Well, I'll just take him back home with me, and we all know how much food I can get down him." The doctor took a stand and told him if he touched my son that he would have the police and children's services on him so fast it would make his head spin. In anger, he turned and said, "Fine, as far as I'm concerned, the kid is dead." He left the hospital and we didn't see him until my son's funeral about a year and a half later. The shape my son was in was devastating; he was three years old and weighed just seventeen pounds. Needless to say, this incident almost killed him.

After he was released from the hospital, in my care, I called my attorney and filed for sole custody of my son. It was granted.

Bringing my son home from the hospital was bittersweet. I was ecstatically happy, but at the same time there was an excruciating pain in my heart due to how ill he was. My fiancé and I tried to make him as comfortable as possible, our home literally looked like a hospital. There was a feeding machine, oxygen tank, dressings and bandages, and many, many medications that had to be given around the clock. This was no easy task by any means. I began by making charts, as not to forget to give him what he needed at the time that he needed it. I wanted him to feel better and I wanted to try to make the quality of his life as awesome as I could. As he began to feel better, we began to feed him baby food along with his supplemental feedings through the nasal gastric tube. I was very pleased when we returned to the doctor for his routine visit. He had gone from seventeen pounds to twenty-three pounds. A day of celebration, he was looking good.

We contacted his father to retrieve his belongings that were left at his home. I spoke with his fiancée; she said we could pick up his stuff and that she would have it ready. When we got there, everything was in big garbage bags. We loaded them into the car and headed for home. I was shocked at what I found as I unpacked his things. They had sent me dirty clothes that smelled so bad I had to wash them two or three times just to get the smell out. A lot of his clothing was moldy and had to be tossed out. They even sent me the dirty gloves that they had used to do empactment treatments on him. This is a treatment that is used when someone is so constipated, that the only way they can go to the bathroom is if someone helps them. I have to say, I never had to do that with my son. There is something in this world called a laxative and it worked very well. Needless to say, I felt terrible, as I had agreed to the arrangement in the first place, but he was with me now and things would be very different.

One of the medications to be administered was Demerol, a pain medication. The hospital was reluctant to let him go home because this is a narcotic. I had to fight the state to let me keep him at home on this medication. It seemed that every time I turned around, I had to fight for something. Now, I was getting stronger, more out-spoken, and more educated by the day. I was determined to keep my son for as long as I could.

In talking with the hospital, they put me in touch with a hospice program. The lady who came to our home was wonderful. She was assigned to our case for as long as we needed her. She would take care of my son when I was at the grocery store, or if my fiancé wanted to take me to dinner. He was safe with her. We also had a visiting nurse who would come once or twice a week to make sure he was doing okay, as well as answer any questions I had. Life was moving along one day at a time, and it seemed we were doing quite well under the circumstances.

My fiancé and I decided on a date for the wedding and proceeded in that direction. We had already bought a house and decided to have another baby. It seemed as though we were doing everything backward, but we were doing it.

Just as the wedding date was approaching, the first time, my son became very ill and had to be hospitalized. I was at home alone with him when he began seizing worse than I had ever seen and then blood began to come from his mouth. He stopped breathing! I called 911 and then screamed for a neighbor to come and help me. He calmed me down as the emergency crew worked on him. I didn't want them to place him on life support, I just wanted them to stop the seizing and control the pain. It seemed that the disease just bounced to the next stage. Upon our arrival in the emergency room, the doctor tried to place him on life support. I begged him not to as the nurses were dragging me out of the room. A Chaplain was just outside the doors and tried to calm me down, I just kept telling him that they didn't understand. I was not trying to keep my son alive, I just wanted him to be comfortable with no pain. If his disease had a treatment or a cure, then yes, put him on life support—but it didn't. Why bring him back to this earth just to endure more pain? I couldn't see the rationale in that. If he was going to die, then let it be his decision, not the doctor's. I pleaded and begged to no avail. I turned my back to that Chaplain and walked about ten steps, turned back around and ran as fast as I could, barreling through the emergency room doors, just as they were getting ready to place the tube in his throat. I said, "Please wait! Listen to me for just a minute." The doctor reluctantly agreed, and I said completely out of breathe, "My son has a rare and fatal disease that will eventually take his life, but you have to understand, there is no treatment or cure for this disease that we or his doctors know of. Everything that you do to him is hit and miss; the one thing we do know for certain is, that he is in a lot of pain. Please! Please don't make him go through anymore. If it was your child, what would you do?" You could have heard a pin drop in that room, and as I looked up the nurse had tears rolling down her face. The doctor turned to me and asked, "What would you like for us to do?" I responded, "Just keep him out of pain and as comfortable as possible." The doctor stated, "You realize that there is a good chance that he will not make it through the night?" I nodded yes. I could no longer control my tears. The doctor said, "Okay."

After he became stable, they moved him to a room in the pediatric unit. He rallied and a few days later we went home. Needless to say, the wedding had to be postponed and another date was set.

This time, it seemed that the disease had taken even more away from my son; he could no longer swallow. Now he was fed completely through the nasal gastric tube. His teeth and lips had to be sponged, and his pain medication was given at a higher dose. Can you imagine going through your life without a drink of water? On top of all of this, his eyesight was beginning to fade. Soon he would be living in the dark. My heart would break daily for his fate and I could find no comfort in this trial, only questions. I was so tired.

As we settled into this new stage, things would stabilize for a time. My fiancé and I began to plan the wedding. We settled on a date in September, rented the hall and paid for the dress. By this time, I was also pregnant. We were so excited. I had purchased a little suit for my son and he looked adorable in it. However, the night before the wedding, his fever began to spike. The doctor said to give him some fever reducer and wait it out. We did and he was fine the next morning. We were married and now life seemed to be getting on the right track, but we needed a miracle for my son. After the wedding, there was no honeymoon. We went back home, opened gifts and settled for a quiet evening. We were a real family now.

A couple of months after the wedding, my son took a dreadful turn for the worst. The doctor admitted him to the hospital to get his pain and seizures under control. The news would be devastating. The Demerol wouldn't work anymore and the only thing they could give him was morphine. We literally lived at the hospital during this time. I went home to shower and eat and that was about it. This hospital visit would last for five months.

During this time, I went into labor on my due date, January 7th, and we checked into the hospital at about 10:30 a.m. We were very excited to begin this great journey. At 1:47 p.m. our daughter made her debut. She was a beautiful dark-haired, blue-eyed baby, weighing in at 8lbs 8 ½ oz and was 21 ¼ inches long. The feelings of joy my husband and I felt were indescribable. We had been through so much, and this seemed like a dream. The tears were flowing like a river. Because of my son's illness, we had genetic counseling and testing before the baby was born, so we knew that she was healthy.

In order for a child to have this type of Leukodystrophy, both parents have to be carriers. My husband wasn't a carrier, and my daughter had a fifty-fifty chance of being a carrier; however, after being tested, she also proved not to be a carrier. No chance of having a baby with this disease, this made us very happy.

My daughter's first ten months of life would be lived out in a hospital beside her brother, as this is where we lived. My son seemed to like his new sister; I would let her sleep in the bed beside him. It seemed to keep him calm. If she cried, he would look from side to side as if to say, what's going on? I would explain to him that she was hungry or her diaper needed to be changed and then he would be fine. He was a typical big brother, very protective, he loved his baby sister.

The pain he endured was so intense that I don't really know how he survived for as long as he did. The nasal gastric tube was no longer effective and we had decided to put in a gastrosomy tube, which is a tube that went straight into his stomach. I had asked the doctor not to take him off his morphine during the surgery, due to withdrawals, and because it was so hard to keep his pain under control. The doctor said no, that the anesthetic would be enough to keep him under and that he wouldn't need the morphine while in surgery. I pleaded and begged but they wouldn't listen. They took him in for surgery, and about ten minutes into it, he woke up. They had to give him an adult dose to put him back to sleep so they could finish the surgery. The doctor said he would be out most of the day; however, by the time he went to recovery, he was awake. The pain was unbearable. They tried to get it under control by giving him doses upon doses of pain medication as well as sedatives and nothing touched the pain. He screamed from about 10:00 a.m. through 11:00 p.m. It got to the point where I could see him scream, but I couldn't hear him anymore, as he had lost his voice. You can imagine my frustration as well as anger at this point, and everyone felt my wrath, and heard it as well. The thing is, the doctors didn't know my son as well as me. I was with him twenty-four-seven. Sometimes, it is good to listen before you respond to the other person and tell them that they don't know what they are talking about. Sure, I'm not a doctor, but at least listen to me so that with my information, and their medical knowledge, an educated decision could have been made. They didn't know how to treat this disease because it was so rare, and as I said, everything they did was a hit and miss guess in most of the circumstances.

As time went on, his veins would blow out and they couldn't give him the morphine in the IV. I remember one time they had to stick him six times. I just cried for him, I felt so helpless. They had to come up with a way to give him morphine through his gastrosomy tube. You would think that this wouldn't be a hard task, but they had to be very careful because the morphine would eat the lining of his stomach. I was very happy when they figured it out and put him on a twenty-four-hour morphine drip that didn't upset his stomach. Okay, now we were on our way, the pain was under control, his stomach tube was in place, the next step? Let's go home, right! Wrong. The state of California said if someone was on morphine, they had to be in a controlled setting, a hospital. However, the hospital he was in didn't want him there anymore because the insurance wouldn't pay until he was released. So now we were facing another dilemma. The hospital put me in touch with some "state" hospitals to check out. I wasn't about to place my son in a "state institution." I couldn't do this, so I fought, and lost. My husband and I went to check out these "hospitals" and there was only one that I would even consider. I set up an appointment and we went to interview the hospital. If they did what they said they would do for my son, I had found a gold mine, and as it turned out, I did. There were a few things I didn't like such as the hospital was an hour and a half away from my home. The other is that we would have to address a bio-ethics committee for a do not resuscitate order (DNR). Over all, the facilities were wonderful and clean. There were about ten children that would be in the same nursery with my son, so his care would be very individualized. At this point, I was willing to try it.

During this transition time, I got a phone call from my son's grandmother. She knew that I was struggling with all of this, and I suppose at this time she was reaching out. I was glad that she had called. There was so much I had to tell her. She told me that she, too, had been questioning why all this was happening and that she was sure I was as well. She found comfort in church and asked me to go with her. Now, I think, by this juncture in the story, you know what my response would be, but reluctantly, and out of politeness, I went. It was so hard for me, all I could do is wonder what that preacher did to his little girls when he went home at night. It was so hard to sit there, and quite frankly, I didn't need it. I had enough to deal with. I didn't need the past creeping in to make me feel worse than I already did and, moreover, I didn't think I could handle it. I just sat there with the preoccupation of my mind writhing in pain. On this night, there wasn't as much preaching, as there was testimony. A lot of these people had been through some very hard and sad times. As I listened, it was evident to me that their hearts were breaking, although, as they continued to speak, I began to see that they weren't unhappy and their hearts were not breaking at all. Quite the contrary, they were filled with joy. I was amazed. I didn't understand, but I definitely wanted to feel what they were feeling. I wanted to be happy; I wanted to get rid of the baggage in my mind. I just didn't know if I could. I didn't know if I could look past the man who was preaching and hear the message, but there was one thing I did know—I couldn't continue living my life as I had been living it. Stuffing everything inside me, growing bitter, and passing blame for my own unhappiness, something happened at that service. I wasn't quite sure what it was, but I decided to return one more time.

This preacher didn't preach about how God was going to "get you" if you didn't do things His way. This message was different; it was a message about love, God's love. As I sat there, I was amazed at what I was feeling. I could literally feel my heart being healed with the love that God was pouring on me during that service. I began to sob, completely broken. I was so tired and beat down, my mind exhausted; I couldn't fight anymore. I was as low as I could get. I knew I wouldn't be able to get up on my own. It's so hard to explain, but for whatever reason, I knew in my heart that I was supposed to be there. When the pastor preached, it was like God was having a conversation with me. He began to answer questions I had about my dad, my mom, and my past. It was a supernatural understanding and for some reason I just knew that everything was going to be all right.

He told me that it was my dad who had made the mistake, not me. He had tried to change him but he wouldn't listen and that He would deal with him. And my mom, she needed healing of her own and when she was ready, He would be there for her, too. As for my son, He just said watch as he completes the mission he was called to do. All these years, how could I trust Him and at what price? God was making me an offer, come back to Him and He would give me peace, the same peace that I had felt as an eight-year-old child.

You would think that my experience would be huge, and a long and drawn out ordeal, but it wasn't. God was very deliberate in what he did for me. I was at the breaking point; I could not have gotten any lower in my life, that's when God made His move. He knew that at this time in my life, I was ready to listen, and that my heart was open to receive all that He had for me. So simple, just like a child's faith, simple.

I am very grateful to my son's grandmother for taking me to that church, she will never know just how much. God used her to save my life. As the years would pass, God and I would become best friends and He would bring me to where I am today, all because of a grandmother who prayed and obeyed His request. I attended and grew in that church for several years, and I have to say the pastor was just that, a pastor. Upright in his standing with God, he showed me that not all men disobey or take advantage of the call on their lives. He helped to restore trust in my heart. It all began with a single invitation to go to church. The power that God has given us to change lives is amazing. I don't think a lot of us realize just how much power we have, if, we will team up with Him.

Upon my son's arrival to the hospital, they had already read his medical records and history. I met with the doctors, nurses and physical therapist, and they had already drafted a plan to improve the quality of life for him, I couldn't believe it! They measured him for a custom-made wheel chair bed that would accommodate only his little body. They would stimulate the senses he had left, which was his hearing. At this point, he couldn't eat with his mouth anymore, and his eyesight was gone. It seemed too good to be true. I was very impressed, however, I still wanted him to come home and I would have to fight for that right.

As my son settled in, I had to work on the more life changing situations for him, such as a do not resuscitate order (DNR). I made an appointment to meet with the bio-ethics committee. The day arrived and I was fully prepared for the task ahead. I didn't want them to place my son on life support, or resuscitate him just so he could come back and experience even more pain. If it was his time to go, I wanted them to let him go. As I got up to make my speech, the faces that stared back at me seemed reasonable and compassionate. I showed them before and after pictures of my son and explained his disease in great length. I was determined to let him die when he and God were ready. I also asked that they let me bring him home on weekends. It didn't take them long to decide, they came back with a unanimous vote. I was very happy, however, there were stipulations; I could take him home on Fridays and would have to return by Sunday afternoon, and the DNR was only good for the acute care unit. What does that mean? It meant that it didn't apply in his nursery; it only applied if he had to go to the regular hospital unit. I was devastated, he would be living in his nursery, how would this help? I talked to the hospital administrator and she said that I would have to go to the state level for that order. She also told me that many had tried, but it had never been done. I was determined! The administrator said if I wanted to fight, she would write me a letter of recommendation, I agreed.

Before my son had entered this hospital, I had the local television station come and write a story on my son to bring awareness to this disease. When writing this letter for the gentleman who was to determine my son's fate, I included a copy of that videotape, as well as before and after pictures of my son. I also wrote him a very heartfelt, but stern, letter telling him about this wonderful little boy and explaining the horrors of this disease. I simply said that if he would let me bring my son home for one week, and if he would come and live in our home for that one week, then whatever the state decided for my son thereafter, I would abide by and I would not fight. They would never hear from me again, but I put in parenthesis: *You will never make it through one day.*

This disease is so cruel and painful that only one family member, outside of my husband, his parents, and me, would come and see him on a regular basis and that was his great grandmother on his dad's side. She would not miss an opportunity to come and see him. Every time he was in the hospital, she was there. She loved him very much. The rest of the family couldn't handle seeing him like this. My family didn't come either, as they all lived out of town or state, nor did they call regularly. However, my husband's parents would prove to be a great support system for me during this time. They would come and see my son whenever they could, and he was accepted as their grandson. They are wonderful people.

It took seven months for a ruling to come back. Because the hospital was an hour and a half away from my home, I went to the hospital every other day and brought my son home every other weekend. On this one day I would get quite a shock. As I entered the door, I would always call out to my son, "Where's my little man?" I would do this so I wouldn't startle him and cause him to seize as I came into the room. He would roll his little eyes back and forth and breathe hard until I touched him. That was his way of telling me, "Hey, Mom, I'm glad you're here." On this particular day, I hadn't made it to the nursery before I saw nurses hurrying, some running, down the hallway, and some of them were crying. It scared me. I thought he might have passed away before I got there so I began to cry! I asked, "What is it?" Very excitedly, they said, "You did it! You did it!" I didn't have a clue as to what they were talking about; it had been seven months. They said the ruling came back and my son got his DNR order! I was so happy! "There's more," they said. I couldn't imagine what. The order was not only for my son, but also for any child who had a terminal illness with very little or no treatment or cure. If his or her parents wanted this, it would be granted depending on the case. We had a victory! I wanted my son to die with dignity, and now it was a reality. Before I fought for this order, I had been told about several children, in this hospital, that had such diseases, and when they would die, by law they had to be resuscitated. One little boy had to die three times before they let him go. This wasn't his parents' wish; they just wanted their little boy to die in peace. All of the nights we pushed my son's bed down the sidewalk to the acute care unit, thinking that this was the night, all the worrying when I wasn't there, it was over; this would no longer be an issue. Sadness and relief filled my heart for I knew what this meant, and I knew what decision had to be made next.

When my son entered the state hospital, he was on about thirty-seven different medications, vitamins, and supplements. It was amazing that he could even stay awake. However, the plan developed by this hospital would prove to be incredible. They took him off anything that they felt was unnecessary, had a duplicate or enhanced effect. I think they cut it by half. My son flourished on this plan. He was more alert and gained quite a bit of weight. He was beginning to look like a normal four-year-old. However, by law there were certain medications that he had to stay on. Although, due to the DNR order, he didn't have to stay on them anymore.

His doctor made an appointment with me to adjust the medications, we obviously kept him on anything that would keep him comfortable and out of pain. I have to say this hospital was so supportive of our decision. They had seen so many children come through their doors who suffered unnecessarily. They were happy that, finally, parents and children would have a choice. When I think of this, I can't help but consider the irony of not so long ago. I had to fight to bring my son into this world, fight to keep him, and now fight for his right to leave this world. Sometimes when I think of all this child went through I can't help but be astounded by his demeanor through it all. It was almost like he knew what he was supposed to do and why he was here. I learned a lot from him.

The doctor told me that he probably wouldn't live a week after the adjustments. It was by far the hardest decision I have ever made and I questioned myself extensively. The alternatives weren't even choices. Because of the medications, his bones had already deteriorated to the point that when he was moved while receiving a bath, the long bone in his leg was broken. They couldn't cast it because his bones were so brittle that it would cause more breaks. His little body was giving out. I felt that just because we could prolong his life through medication, didn't necessarily mean we should. I wasn't in the habit of playing God and didn't have any desire to, and besides, you have to ask yourself at some point, "Who am I doing this for?" Prolonging his life would be selfish on my part. I didn't want him to suffer anymore. I had made my decision and I felt peace in making it.

You know, as I look at this trial in my life, I can clearly see God at work. Several incidents that occurred during these two and half years of illness clearly show that God was in the midst of it all. Remember the nurse in the hall at the beginning of the illness who said, "You can let this disease take advantage of you, or you can take advantage of this disease?" I believe that she was an angel, what other explanation could there be? I didn't know what that meant at the time nor did I care. Look at what God did not only for my son but also for many others at this time and in the future to come, all because we chose to take advantage of this disease.

It was a beautiful fall day when I awoke with a heavy heart, and as I tried to do my daily duties, I told my husband that I didn't feel right. I felt like something was wrong. He had told me to call the hospital and I told him I couldn't, I was afraid of what they might say. He continued to encourage me to call. Because I had a cold, I couldn't visit my son, as they wouldn't let anyone in the nursery if they were sick. Finally, I called. They said that he was fine, that he was rallying, he was doing great. So why did I feel like my heart was going to break? I continued to go about my day with this knot in my stomach. My husband, a restaurant manager, was getting ready for work. He asked, "Why don't you and the baby come to the restaurant in a little while and have dinner and then we will come home together?" I nodded, "Okay." He left for work and I called the hospital again, and again they told me he was fine, he was doing great. The time came, for the baby and me, to go to the restaurant but my mind was so preoccupied that I don't remember how I got there. I just remember being in the car and a bright light flashing in my face, and the next thing I knew, we were sitting in the parking lot of the restaurant. I got the baby out of the car and we went in to eat. As I sat down at the table there were all these words going through my head. It was like God was saying write this down, so I did, on several napkins. I placed them in the diaper bag, and ate dinner with my family.

When my husband and I got home, we put the baby to bed and I sat down at the computer to type what I had written on the napkins. When I was done, I read what God had given me. I was stunned, but in a peaceful way. I knew my son was going to die that night and I told my husband this. He just looked at me, shocked, and said, "How do you know?" I said, " Read this." As he did, you could see the blood run from his face. He didn't know what to say to me, he just sat there in silence. After a few minutes he got up and said, "It's late, I'm going to bed." I told him I would be along in a bit. As I sat there staring at the paper, I didn't know what to do, so I just sat there. Finally I got up to go to bed, the television was on, but the station had gone off the air so it was just snow on the screen. I turned it off, and as I got in bed, I felt like someone had lifted a heavy weight off my mind and body. I felt as though for the first time since this started, I could take a deep breath. I turned to my husband and said, "Well, I guess the hospital will be calling any minute now." All I could see in the darkness was the whites of his eyes; I think I freaked him out. It was about 1:45 in the morning. As I lay there in the darkness, I couldn't sleep for I knew the call was coming. Sure enough, the phone rang. My husband and I sat up in bed. I went to answer the phone and he followed. The voice on the other end asked for me. I said this is she, and they said this is the hospital and we are calling to let you know that your son has just passed away. I said, "Okay," and then dropped to my knees as my husband grabbed me to break the fall. He wrapped his arms around me as we huddled on the floor, sobbing.

The car ride to the hospital seemed to take forever. We had to pull to the side of the road so I could vomit. I didn't know how I was going to be able to handle this. All the thoughts running through my mind, the pictures of his frail and lifeless body were more than I could take. How could I live my life without him, what would I do, how could I go on?

I don't think there is any amount of preparation that will prepare you for something like this. I mean, we knew he was going to die, we had two and a half years to get used to the idea, but still, I think, no, I know that somewhere deep inside, even though you know it's coming, it doesn't register until it actually happens. So how can you possibly prepare?

Once we arrived, the doctor talked with me and told me that according to their clock, he passed away at 1:49 a.m. He proceeded to tell me how it happened. The cause of death, cardiac and respiratory arrest, he said he wasn't in any pain; he just simply went to sleep. As I took a deep breath, they took me in to see him. He was still in his nursery, in his own bed, he looked so peaceful as his frail and lifeless body lay there with his arm around his teddy bear. It looked as if he was just sleeping, my little angel. Finally, he really is at peace, no more pain, no suffering, no medication, nothing, just peace.

As I sat in the family waiting room, I remembered the words that God had given me just hours earlier, and I found comfort knowing that God loved me enough to allow my son to tell me good-bye in such a revealing way. These are the words that He gave me:

"A Mother's Vow"

As I was walking through Heaven on this special day,
I heard a call that directed toward my way,
So I stepped out upon this cloud so fluffy white,
And I saw my mommy praying in the night,

And she said,
"As I sat and watched my baby play,
I never knew in all this world he'd be taken away,
I had such hopes, such dreams, and such fears,
But I never once dreamed there'd be such tears."

And The Lord said,
"Come to Me, come into these arms and see your guiding light."
He said,
"Come to Me and see the path you were sent to trod."
He said,
"Come into these arms so safe from harm,
And then, my child, you will be alright."

"Dear Lord, I loved this child with all my might,
And I always prayed that he would turn out right,
But, dear Lord, you came upon my child one night,
And said, 'I need him to be a guiding light.'"

And The Lord said,
"Come to Me, come into these arms and see your guiding light."

He said,
"Come to Me and see the path you were sent to trod."
He said,
"Come into these arms so safe from harm,
And then, my child, you will be alright."

So reluctantly she broke the vow she'd made,
To keep me safe and loved in a special way,
And with her head held up ever so high,
My mommy struggled through the pain and strife.

"Dear Lord," I prayed, on that special day,
"Please come down and take my baby away,
No more pain, no suffering or fears,
Please, God, come and take away our tears."

So on this cloud way up in the sky,
I turned and told my mommy good-bye,
And while walking and talking
With my Jesus hand-in-hand,
Oh, Mommy, I am now your strong little man.

And The Lord said,
"Come to Him, come into His arms and see your guiding light."
He said,
"Come to Him and see the path I was sent to trod."
He said,
"Come into His arms so safe from harm,
And then, my child, you will be alright."

"And then, Mommy, I know you'll be alright."

Every time I read this, I stand amazed at how much God really does love me. He didn't have to give this to me, yet He knew that I needed this comfort. He wanted me to know that my son was finally okay.

As I write, I am reminded of yet another miracle. During our interview process of this hospital, we met a nurse who was celebrating five years of being cancer free. She was a wonderful lady with a great personality, and I was glad that she would be one of many caring for my son. Upon my son's admittance, we would find out that the cancer had returned in this nurse. So the next time we saw her, she had no hair due to the chemotherapy, however, she continued to have an upbeat attitude. She had the type of personality that was contagious; you just had to be happy, she insisted on it. Although we were saddened by her news, we remained confident that she would survive this. Some time later, she told us that they had run some tests and that they couldn't find any cancer, and we were overjoyed. A prayer answered. She and I became good friends and I depended on her a lot for support through my son's illness. She was always there. The night my son passed away, she was working. As the time got closer for him, she did exactly what she knew I would have done. She said that late in the night, his breathing was becoming more and more delayed. She was reasonably sure that this was his time to go, so she put a fresh T-shirt on him, combed his hair, brushed his teeth, and placed his favorite bear right where he liked it, under his arm next to his face. She then told the other nurses that this was it and not to bother him, it was his time to go. One of the other nurses said if she hadn't been there, they might have tried to resuscitate him. Even with the order, some of the nurses didn't think that they could let him go without intervention. I was very grateful to my friend, as I'm sure my son was. She stood strong and made sure that he was able to die in peace and dignity. It amazes me still that God places people very strategically in our lives at just the right time and in the capacity in which we need them. After my son passed away, her cancer returned and early in the next year she also passed away. It was a sad time for us all.

On the day of my son's memorial service, God showed me yet another miracle. I wanted to have a small service in the funeral chapel, just family and close friends. However, when I prayed about this, I changed my mind and had it in our church and had our pastor oversee the service. Now, I was able to see just what God meant and how my son's life affected others. The hospital put everyone who had ever taken care of my son on the hospital bus and sent them to his service. Also, people who had read his obituary, people who we had met in a hospital, or in passing, came to his memorial service. As I looked around that church, I was astounded by the number of lives this little four-and-a-half-year-old baby had touched. This was a child who couldn't walk, talk, or see, and look at what he accomplished; his mission was becoming clear to me. It has to make you think, with all our faculties, how many lives could we change? To this day, he is still changing lives. How? After my son's death, I didn't go back to work in my related field. Instead, I opened a daycare and later a preschool, which I operated for many years. Why? The decision came after careful thought and conversation with my husband. Together, we sat down and looked at our daughter, who was ten months old when my son passed away. We realized that you couldn't take children for granted. They could be here today and gone tomorrow, just that quick. I wanted to make an impact in the lives of children, I wanted them to know that they were special and that they could accomplish anything they set their minds to. We made our decision knowing in our hearts that we wanted to make a difference in our world, starting with the beginning of life, children. This set me on a path that would not only be rewarding, but life changing. Years later the words that God gave me that special night became so revealing in the way I would live my life.

The memorial service was over and my mom had invited me to come and stay with her for a while, and I agreed. I thought that getting away from the environment would help me to heal; however, I was having great difficulty letting him go. The grief of a child is something that I think on any scale you would describe, really couldn't come close to describing how you feel at all.

One night while at my mom's, I awoke abruptly, sat up in bed as if I had slept all night and was ready to get up, but it was the middle of the night. As I sat in the darkness, I looked over to a wall that had an old antique cabinet with a medieval times portrait painted on it. As I gazed at this portrait, I saw my son's face smiling back at me, his beautiful blue eyes twinkling. I was taken back by this event and was very afraid. I lay back down and placed the covers over my head, thinking, *I am losing it!* I didn't dare tell anyone for fear that they may think I needed to be sedated or worse, hospitalized.

Upon my return home, similar events would take place. I was giving my daughter a bath. She had asked for her favorite toy, so I ran into the living room to get it. I would have to pass by the laundry room, as well as my daughter's bedroom. As I passed back by on my way to the bathroom, I saw a child sitting in my daughter's room. I thought, *This is odd, how did she get out of the tub and into her room so fast?* But as I backed up, I saw my son sitting there playing with one of his favorite toys that we had gotten him the Christmas before the illness took over his body. He looked up at me, and again, with those twinkling blue eyes smiled at me. My reaction was anything but normal. I got my daughter dressed and we immediately went to the church to talk with our pastor. He explained to me that sometimes when we don't let go right away, a spirit might linger to let us know that they are okay. I took comfort in this explanation and so when I got home, I began to pray that I would see my son again, only this time, I gave God some specifics. I asked him to open the Heavens and let me see my son run across a big green pasture. I never got to see him run. The Lord tenderly touched my heart and said, "Tammie, if I open the Heavens and let you see him run across a big green pasture, you would never want to stay on earth." I just sat there in awe as I cried for what seemed like hours. After this cleansing time, I felt a peace that I could not understand or describe. I never saw my son again. Once more, God showed His love for me through this ordeal, and this would prove to be a relationship that would grow to be a very deep and abiding faith. Through all the things that I had felt as a child, and now as an adult, God was daily melting away the pain of everything that had happened as He poured His love onto me.

Time was bringing healing, and life began to take on a normal routine. I opened my doors to the care of other children and concentrated heavily on the life of my daughter. God knew exactly what He was doing when He gave her to me, especially at the time that He did. He knew that I couldn't handle not being a mom. My daughter helped me through a lot of difficult times and she was and is a joy to have in my life.

When my daughter was almost two years old, my husband and I decided to try for another baby. Our hearts were yearning for a son; however, just as long as the baby is healthy would be just fine with us. As we began this journey, we would find that it wasn't as easy as with our daughter. After a time, we decided to try fertility drugs and with great success, we were pregnant. We were so excited! I had prayed and asked God to give us a son, and at the same time, I was very specific. I wanted a dark-haired little boy with dark eyes and dark skin. My husband's mother is part Indian and she has beautiful olive skin, so I didn't feel I was asking for something unreasonable. I took "being specific in your prayers" to heart. We began the doctor visits with great enthusiasm. The first ultra-sound was awesome. I remember thinking, *Life doesn't get any better than this.* The pregnancy appeared to be going fine, but it would be short-lived. One night when I went to the restroom, I noticed that I had begun bleeding; we called the doctor immediately. He set up an emergency ultra-sound at his office. I cannot tell you the fear that was in my heart as I lay on that table waiting for the doctor to speak. As my husband held my hand, we tried to prepare ourselves for the worst. When the doctor spoke, he explained, as he showed us on the ultra-sound screen, that it appeared that we may have had twins. One was weaker than the other and it was apparent that one might have died. The doctor explained that the babies were not identical twins, thus each had their own amniotic sac. That is why one could survive even if the other didn't. It is so hard to explain how we felt—we were losing one baby, but at the same time, we also were having a baby. Over the next several weeks, there would be endless ultra-sounds and doctor appointments. The doctor put me on strict bed rest until he felt the baby was out of the danger. At every ultra-sound appointment, we would watch as the other baby, or "fetal tissue," dissolved and my body reabsorbed it. It was what they call "Vanishing Birth Syndrome." It was a bittersweet feeling to say the least. Just when we thought everything was okay, it appeared that the dissolution of the "fetal tissue" became a cyst that came between the placenta and the other baby, threatening to rupture the amniotic sac, thus causing us to lose the other baby as well. It was so stressful, not knowing what to expect from day to day. Finally, after thirteen ultra-sounds, the ordeal was over, the cyst had dissolved completely and the baby was fine. The technician asked if we would like to know the sex of the baby, and after all that we had been through, we felt that this would be a great reward. When we agreed, he said, "It's a boy." We were so overjoyed that we could hardly contain ourselves. We were going to have a son!

The rest of the pregnancy, unfortunately, did not go without incident. It was determined that I had a chemical imbalance. Too many hormones, my body would have episodes of blindness in one eye followed by complete paralysis on one side of my body. And when I would speak, it would appear that I had been drinking quite heavily. These episodes would last from one to two hours at a time. It was frightening, it began when I was about six months pregnant and didn't end until I stopped nursing.

My son didn't want to come out on his own, so after being more than two weeks overdue, my doctor decided to induce labor. He said he should be an average size baby, but, if he were over nine pounds, they would have to do a caesarean.

The day we all waited for finally came. I was in labor for five hours when our son decided to make his entrance, and what a grand entrance it was. My husband was the first to see him as he cut the cord. The doctor handed him his new son. The tears in his eyes; the look on his face is one that will forever be embedded in my mind. Our son weighed in at 9 lbs 12 oz, and was 21 ½ inches long. He had dark hair, dark eyes, and bright pink skin, which would prove to be dark as he grew. My prayer was answered in every way, and I didn't have to have a caesarean—many stitches, but not a caesarean. We were so happy; God had smiled on our family. The road was rough getting him here, but it made us cherish him all the more.

As he was passed from dad to mom to sister to grandmother to grandfather, we all felt blessed to have such a beautiful and healthy baby. My husband's parents were wonderful; through everything we went through in the past right up to the present, they were so supportive.

His big sister was more than pleased to have a little brother. She was so excited we could hardly contain her. She wanted to hold him all the time, as well as play with him like he was one of her baby dolls. Life was good.

Time seemed to pass with great swiftness. We were busy with two children, and just life in general. When our son was about a year old, my husband took a job in Seattle, working for my stepfather. It was a culture shock from California and, I have to say, I was not happy. I wanted to go home, I did not want to be there, and I cried that whole first year.

Upon our arrival we started looking for a church to attend, and it wasn't easy finding one like we had been attending in California. We tried several and were getting frustrated. We decided to visit a church about a mile from our home. You know, it's funny, sometimes the place you belong is actually the place in which you are already sitting. Anyway, we decided to try this church but when we got there, the service had already begun. We didn't want to go in late, so we wrote down the service times from the sign and decided to try again that evening. In the meantime, we had lunch and familiarized ourselves with the surroundings of the community. During the course of the day, we had gotten into a heated discussion about the discipline of our children. My husband is the passive one in this area, and upon our arrival of the church, we agreed to disagree.

When we entered the sanctuary, the atmosphere was so warm, it was like God had wrapped His arms around us and said, "You're home." We sat near the back of the church and just watched as the service began. The praise and worship was awesome, it was not like anything we had ever experienced. You could definitely feel the presence of God in this place. It got even better. When the pastor got up to preach, the first thing he said was, "…and tonight we are going to talk about discipline of your children." My husband and I just looked at each other in disbelief as he jabbed me in the arm with his elbow. He bent down and said, "You know someone here, don't you?" I just looked at him in shock and said, "Excuse me?" Who did I know? I had never seen any of these people before in my life. Boy, oh boy, if God wasn't reading our mail, then I don't know who was. I think God was telling us in a very comical way that we were right where we belonged. We attended this church for almost ten years until we moved to Texas.

Because of this church, I started to feel connected to the community. I began to make friends by attending a women's Bible study. The teaching was phenomenal; it was just that, teaching. The pastor expected you to have your Bible every time you entered into a service. If you didn't, you had better sit toward the back, because if he didn't see a Bible, he would ask you why, right then. He expected you to follow along and look up every scripture that he directed you to. I have a lot of respect for this pastor, one reason being he always said, "Don't take my word for it, look it up for yourself. I am human and I could make a mistake." He just wanted people to be saved and to know the truth, God's truth. I learned my Bible from cover to cover at this church, and this is the place I called home.

As time passed, we would find ourselves parents-to-be once again. Our daughter was almost five and our son almost two. We were ready and excited, as we adored children. We started once again with the regular doctor appointments. Everything seemed to be going near perfect with this pregnancy and life was good. We had scheduled our first ultra-sound to find out the due date. My husband took the day off work and we were on our way. When the technician began the ultra-sound, he didn't say much and we thought that was odd. Finally, he stood up and said, I need to get your doctor, I'll be right back. Once again my husband and I found ourselves hand-in-hand preparing for the worst. The doctor came in and, after acknowledging us, sat where the technician had. As he spoke, my heart dropped. I felt as though I was in a tunnel and unable to hear clearly. As I began to cry, he told us that our baby had died. He didn't know why, and that sometimes these things happen. He told us that I would more than likely miscarry and that we should let my body do this on its own, as he didn't want to do anything invasive unless it was necessary. So, he sent me home to wait. You know, I just didn't understand, I didn't understand why we had to go through yet another trial. I was almost four months along at this point and I really, really didn't want to have to do this. Once again I began to question God, how could this happen?!

A week or so went by and I had not yet passed the baby. I began to feel weak and started having fainting spells. We called the doctor, and he informed us that the baby had become toxic and was poisoning my body. I would need an emergency D and C to take the baby. On our way to the hospital, I couldn't even look at my husband, I felt as though I let him down. So much had happened during our married life, was it too much to ask for a complication-free life?

Upon our arrival they prepared me for surgery. Thank God for drugs, they gave me a sedative right from the start to calm me down. When I woke up it was over, the doctor said he had sent the "fetal tissue" to the lab for a pathology report and he would let me know of the results in about a week or so. I left feeling so empty and right then I decided, no more children; it was too painful. I had two beautiful children and that's all I needed, and I knew I just couldn't do this anymore. Of course, at this point, I hadn't discussed the subject with my husband.

About a week later the doctor called with the results of the pathology report, and the questions I had been asking God were answered. My doctor told me that the baby was a little girl and that she had so many birth defects, that even if she had made it to term, she would have never survived outside the womb. I was sad, but relieved. I knew I didn't want to go through another life-threatening illness with a child, just to watch them die. I know God had a plan for my oldest son and a lot of life lessons were learned, but I didn't think I could survive it all over again. A blessing in disguise, I was able to love and cherish my children and other people's even more. I felt that God was showing me how precious and fragile life is, and that we need to get busy and do as much to influence our world as we can with the life that He has given us.

Once again, only time would heal the wound. However, it wasn't long before my husband would bring up the subject of another baby. I would be very firm in this area, as we would have countless conversations and heated discussions about it.

One such conversation got me thinking: he said that I couldn't live my life in fear and that if we didn't try again, that fear would overcome me. As I thought about this, I knew he was right. This fear would probably spill over to my children and affect the future of my grandchildren, or lack there of as the case might be. So, I said okay. Three months later, we tried again. I became pregnant and once again we were off and running to the doctor. Again this seemed to be a picture-perfect pregnancy. I held my breath, as did my husband, at our first ultra-sound appointment. They found absolutely no problems, but just to be sure, they would send me to a renowned ultra-sound specialist. He walked me through the test and it was awesome. I had never had one that was quite so sensitive. He counted every vertebra in the baby's back, checked all the chambers in the heart, counted the fingers, toes, eyes, ears, nose and mouth, and gave me a front seat view to the kidneys and all pertinent organs. He then turned to me and asked, "Do you want to know the sex of the baby?" I said, "Yes!" He said, "It's a girl." We were overjoyed! A little girl. Who would she look like? What would we name her?

The pregnancy progressed beautifully with the exception of gestational diabetes, which was controlled by diet, but other than that, I was almost six months along and doing great!

Because of my lung and sinus disease, I had regular appointments to keep track of the diseases to make sure everything was as it should be. On a routine yearly check-up with my ear, nose, and throat specialist, he found a small lump on my neck, about the size of a kidney bean. He said it was probably nothing to worry about, but I should get it checked out. He didn't seem very concerned, so I wasn't concerned; however, that would change quite rapidly. About a week later, I was looking in the mirror and it had grown from the kidney bean size to the size of a quarter. I immediately called my pulmonary specialist, which was also an internal medicine specialist. He made an appointment for me immediately. Once examined, he decided that further testing was necessary and, because I was six months pregnant, this would present some problems. He decided on an ultra-sound of the neck. He sent me across the street the same day for the test. When it was over, my husband and I went home, this was on a Friday. The test came back that same day with less than preferable results and a biopsy was scheduled for the following Monday. The results of that test would change my life forever, again!

The test determined that I had a rapidly growing tumor in my thyroid. My doctor sent me to a specialist in this area. After more testing, he determined that surgery was inevitable and should be immediate. We were sent spinning. I couldn't have surgery, I was pregnant! He informed us that we could wait until the baby was born, but that I probably wouldn't make it, and he wasn't so sure the baby would either. We had asked if we could wait a few more weeks until the baby was more developed—because of the diabetes, her lungs weren't anywhere near ready. If she was born now, the odds were that she wouldn't make it. He told us that we could wait, but again, he wasn't so sure that I would make it. His only choice for us was now. Later would mean a baby and no mother, or no baby and no mother. If we did the surgery now, we would be taking a chance that the baby would be born, and we knew she wasn't ready and what the outcome might be. Our lives were in utter chaos. I wanted to scream. My husband and I agonized over this decision. What should we do?

The first thing we did was contact our church and they began to pray for our situation. Our pastor and the church were so supportive. He told us that God would take care of us. All I had to do is believe. The decision had to be made right away, and after weighing all the information, we decided to have the surgery now. We had to take a step in faith and believe that God would prevail, that our baby and myself would be okay. From the time they found the tumor to the surgery date was two weeks. One of the thoughts that crossed my mind was this baby obviously has a tremendous purpose—why else would Satan try to take her life?

As we prepared for the unexpected, you can imagine our anxiety. My gynecologist made arrangements to be in the operating room to monitor the baby. The surgeon was the best in Washington State; we were in good hands. My husband was joined, in the waiting room, by my mom and stepfather. The surgery took about three hours and all went well. They had called my husband earlier and told him that everything went fine and that we were on our way to recovery. They gave him my room number and said the doctor would come and talk to him later.

Meanwhile, in recovery, I began to wake up and the first words I heard were, "We are losing the baby!" I panicked and began to cry as the doctor said, "Let's get her prepped for a caesarean!" I just kept saying no! No! No! They were trying to call my gynecologist so he could come back to the operating room. Because the surgery had gone so well, he had already gone back to his office.

When he got the call, he tried to come back, but someone had hit his car in the parking garage. He had to run six blocks up hill to get back to me. As they were wheeling me into the operating room, he busted through the doors and said, "Okay, people, let's not do something we all are going to regret." He started giving orders and people were running around like ants. He said, "Let's get an ultra-sound in here to see what this little girl is doing." So everyone took a breath and waited as he ran the test. The anesthetic was catching up with her and her heart rate dropped into the 70s from the 180s. He told the nurses to perform fetal massage on the outside of my tummy to wake the baby up. As three nurses massaged briskly, she began to move as we watched her on the ultra-sound screen. Over time, about forty minutes to an hour or more, she was getting mad, we could see her kicking and throwing her little arms about. She was awake and her heart rate began to rise. Finally, she was out of danger and doing great. I'll never forget how my doctor busted through those doors and saved my baby's life. He was definitely her knight in hospital scrubs armor.

When my husband got back from lunch, they couldn't find me. Because of the complications, they sent me to the neonatal unit instead of a regular room, so they could monitor the baby.

Needless to say, this frightened my family.

Everyone was waiting anxiously to hear the news about my condition. My doctor told us that the cancer was in my left thyroid and had spread to my vocal cords, vocal cord nerves, and down my esophagus. He said had I waited, his worst fear would have been confirmed, I wouldn't have made it.

In explaining the surgery to me, the doctor said that the incision would be about three inches, and depending on where the cancer was located, he couldn't guarantee that I would ever speak again.

By the time they were done, the incision was seven inches across my neck. They took out both sides of the thyroid and they had to scrape my vocal cords and the nerves, not to mention the esophagus. Blessed? You bet! Was God looking out for my baby and me? Absolutely!

Several doctors told me that if you had to have a cancer, that this would be the one to have. It is highly treatable with a 95% cure rate with radiation treatment. However, mine was very aggressive, and they were hoping it was because of the pregnancy. Now I just had to complete my pregnancy, have a healthy baby, wait six weeks, have radiation treatment and then go about life as normal, right? Right!

Recovery was slow to say the least. They placed me on thyroid medication and I began to feel better. Trips to the hospital three times a week for stress tests were a must. They were monitoring the baby very closely and she was doing great. My gynecologist had discussed delivery options with me and we decided on an epidural. He explained that because my body had already gone through so much trauma, he felt this would be the least stressful and it would get me up and about quicker. I hate needles and didn't relish the idea, but I agreed.

About two weeks before the due date, I went to the hospital for a stress test and everything was fine, the baby was strong with lots of movement, a great report. On the way home, my son had fallen asleep in his car seat, so I picked him up to take him upstairs to his bed. He was a big boy and while carrying him I pulled the round ligament muscles in my stomach. I called the doctor and he said if the pain didn't stop in an hour, that I would have to return to the hospital for another stress test. The hospital was an hour away and I really didn't want to drive back, however, when he called back, he told me to return. I called my husband and told him what had happened. I asked him to meet me at the hospital; he agreed.

Upon my arrival, I went to labor and delivery and they hooked me up to the monitor. I was there for about an hour when the doctor said, "Okay, no contractions so I'm going to let you go home, but first I'm going to check you. I don't want you to deliver an Interstate 5 baby." I was in favor of that since my previous deliveries were pretty fast. My doctor didn't know what to expect from this one. When he checked me, he was shocked to find that I was almost four centimeters dilated. He said if I walked around and got to a complete four that they would keep me. I said no problem. In the meantime, he said he had a soccer game to go to. I told him to go ahead and we would deliver this baby when he got back. I didn't really want to have the baby on this day because it was my son's third birthday; I wanted him to have his own day. So, I waited to climb the stairs and walk the halls. Later, my doctor called to say he was on his way back to the hospital. The doctor on call said I was seven centimeters with no contractions; this was normal for me. My doctor said go ahead and break her water. The contractions hit just as he was walking into my room. He said that is enough, let's get the epidural ready. Once the epidural was in, she was born in about a half an hour. Three hours start to finish.

She was beautiful! She had dark hair and big blue eyes and weighed in at 7 lbs 11 ozs and was 21 ¼ inches long. She didn't really cry when she came out, she would just lie there looking around. They had to stick her little foot six times before she would cry. She was a good baby, very content, very happy. My husband and I just looked at each other in amazement. It doesn't matter how many babies you have, it is a miracle every time. She was the only one out of all my children who looked like me. We went home the next day and settled into our life with baby. Her big sister became the second mom. Her brother was very protective, he watched her like a hawk, making sure that we didn't forget her when we went anywhere and making sure she didn't cry unnecessarily. He was so cute. They welcomed her with warmth and great excitement. We were so happy, another hurdle conquered, a victory won.

The next eight weeks were amazing. With everything that we had just gone through, I found myself paying more attention to the little things in life. A smile, an innocent giggle, watching your children as they play, taking a picture in your mind of every detail, you tend to listen a little more intently to what they are saying, and you don't put them off when they are begging for your attention. Life's little rewards become very significant.

The time came for me to have the radiation treatment. I wasn't happy, even though I knew it had to be done. It was just so hard; I had to go off my medication, which makes you feel like you can't function. It doesn't matter how much sleep you get, you stay tired—and the baby, she was just a newborn, eight weeks was not enough time for me, I wanted to wait. The doctors insisted because the cancer had been so aggressive, they wanted to make sure I was going to be around for a long time, which I appreciated.

Treatment would consist of three days in isolation at the hospital, no visitors, not even the doctor or nurses. However, my husband would convince them to let him in for ten seconds, long enough for him to toss me a box of chocolate and say I love you. He was then ushered out promptly. All my meals were served on Styrofoam and everything in the room was wrapped in plastic including the toilet seat and faucet. There were signs in the room that said if I removed the plastic, anything that I touched would have to be disposed of in an incinerator. I was just a little intimidated. However, the greatest intimidation would come when they actually administered the radiation. The doctor came wrapped in a lead apron, lead gloves and a mask. Here I am sitting in my nice little hospital gown with its built in air conditioner and he was clothed in lead. Yeah, this was just a little intimidating. I was actually somewhat frightened. If they were taking all these precautions for themselves, what was this drug going to do to me? Of course, I really didn't have any alternatives at this point, this situation really played with my mind. I told my husband that I now knew how the people felt in Bible times who had leprosy. I had been through a lot of physical pain in my life, but this kind of pain was different. It was worse for me, I felt so alone.

As the doctor wheeled the cart in, I watched very carefully as he removed the lid, not knowing what to expect. I saw a layer of lead and another lid. He removed that lid and again another layer of lead and another lid. Finally, he pulled out this very small vial with what looked like water in it. He said, "Okay," as he penetrated the top and placed in it a straw-like tube. "Drink up!" I almost vomited just from the thought. I drank it and it tasted like stale water. He then took out this meter gun that measures how much radiation your letting off. He points it at me as he heads for the door, he stands there for a moment and then he moves to the rooms on either side of me to make sure the levels are safe for others. This was repeated several times throughout my stay. When I was no longer emitting dangerous levels, they let me go home; however, there would be strict instructions.

Upon my return home, my couch would be wrapped in plastic, I would have to rinse the shower at least twice, flush the toilet twice, wash my clothes by themselves at least three times, eat off disposable plates and use disposable toothbrushes. I couldn't be within ten feet of my children and could not sleep in the same bed as my husband. It was hard for my children to understand why I couldn't hug or hold them. My mother and my husband's mother would trade off on the care of my family. For this I was very grateful. I don't know what I would have done had they not been there. It made the children feel more comfortable as well.

This was an extremely difficult time for me. I couldn't hold my baby for at least ten days and then I would have to return to the doctor to see how much radiation I was still emitting. I told him I had to hold my baby and he said that my body was emitting low amounts except for the neck area. He said it was safe amounts for everyone, except the baby, because she was so tiny, so he gave me two lead neck aprons that totaled about twenty pounds. I could use these to hold her at arms length. It would be another ten days before I could hold her without the lead aprons. This was so hard, as I would have to watch others take care of her and when she cried. I couldn't go to her and cuddle her. Mothers are not equipped to be away from their newborns like this. I was so glad when this part of my life was over. Over the next couple of years, there would be regular tests and follow-up scans to make sure my body was behaving. It was a very difficult two years due to a roller coaster ride with my thyroid medication. They would have to take me off the medication for four weeks before a scan, so I gained a lot of weight each time I went off the meds, a total of about ninety pounds. However, I lost it all once they declared me cancer free—it took a few years, but I did lose it.

It's been almost two years now and our baby daughter is thriving. Her hair has turned a golden blonde and little ringlets hang all over her head. She is an absolute joy, with big blue eyes and a contagious smile. We have been blessed with three absolutely gorgeous children—of course I am a little partial. The kids are busy doing what kids do, trying to prove their independence in a variety of ways. The baby was no different. We started the potty training process; however, we were not having very much success. She began having urinary tract infections. I took her to the doctor and they put her on antibiotics. Her doctor explained that little girls often will get an infection or two, so, we really were not alarmed. Over the course of the next few months, the infections would become out of control. Her pediatrician recommended a urologist for us to see. After testing, he determined that she had a little dip in her urethra and that the urine was sitting there, getting stagnant and then backwashing into her bladder, thus causing an infection. He recommended going in and repairing this little defect and also to perform exploratory surgery just to make sure that everything else was fine. It would be a fairly simple procedure, they would do it in outpatient services and we could take her home that day. We were okay with this.

The day came for the surgery and we weren't worried—a little anxious, we just wanted it over. It wasn't long into the surgery before the doctor came out and said, "Mrs. Rizan, we need to take a walk." I began to panic, I knew what that meant. Flashes from the past began to enter my mind and I said, "What do you mean?" He said, "Let's go to my office." He showed me her x-rays and basically said that during some point of her development in the womb, she did not develop properly and that she would need reconstructive surgery to correct the defect. "Exactly what is the defect?" I asked. He said, "The tubes that transport the urine from the kidneys to the bladder were located in the wrong place, causing the urine to backwash into the kidneys, causing them to be infected as well as the bladder." This was very serious; if we didn't or couldn't correct this, she could lose both her kidneys by the time she was a teen. "What do we do now?" I asked. He gave me the name of a doctor at a children's hospital that specializes in this type of surgery. We made an appointment to see him right away.

Upon our arrival, I could tell he was a good doctor. He was soft-spoken and very gentle. He drew us a picture and explained what was going on with our daughter; he told us that he had done hundreds of procedures like this and was confident that she would be just fine. Given our history, I couldn't help but be a little apprehensive. He said that once the surgery was over, we would have to help her to train her body to tell her brain when it was time to go to the bathroom. We definitely had quite a chore ahead of us.

One of the first things we did was call our church and have them start praying. I praise God for this church; they were always there when we needed them. They helped with everything from praying to counseling to bringing meals during hospital stays or illnesses. They were wonderful through every trial that they went through with us, and this one was no different.

The day came for the surgery; I'll never forget that day. As we walked our daughter down the hall and into the room where they prepped her, she was so happy, no fear. They asked her what her favorite flavor was and she said, "Cherry!" They gave her the mask that they had coated with her favorite flavor, to put on her face. As she fell asleep, I felt as though I would faint right there on the floor. I just remember praying profusely that God would bring her out of the surgery with no complications. Two hours later, she was in recovery and doing very well. The doctor said everything went fine and now it was just a wait and see time. She was in the hospital for a week; they didn't want to release her until she could urinate on her own. They had inserted a tube into her abdomen that went right into her bladder. She had a bag strapped to her leg where the urine was collected. It had a shut-off valve on it that, when turned off, would force her body to urinate on its own. At least that was the plan. The doctor told us it was like jump-starting her kidneys and that with most kids, this wasn't a problem. However, there was a percentage of children who would have to wear the bag for the rest of their lives. The day came for her to be released and she still hadn't gone to the bathroom on her own. I was getting a little anxious to say the least. The doctor wasn't happy about the progress, but decided to let her go home anyway with a follow-up appointment in his office the next week. We took her home with as much optimism as we could muster. She began doing all the things she normally did in spite of the bag. She wasn't going to let that get in her way; it was quite inspiring. We had been home for almost a week now and had gotten ourselves back into our "normal" routine. When she would go down for a nap, I would turn the valve off and pray that this would be the day.

I had been sitting on the couch reading when she woke up and came into the living room. She was rubbing her eyes and crying, I went to her and she said through her tears, "Mommy, I pee pee the bed." I started crying and screaming and jumping around. I think I scared her pretty bad. I told her it was okay as I hugged and kissed her. I also woke up my son and my daycare children during this fit of excitement. They all began to jump around and celebrate with me. Our home was a big family to all who entered our doors and it was obvious that my baby was well loved. We called my husband and told him the great news. I can't tell you how many tears of joy that were shed that day, but I know we probably could have filled a lake. I picked her up and just held her for the longest time, all the while thanking God for healing my baby. I called the doctor and he was overjoyed. He made an appointment for us to come in and remove the bag. We were ecstatic, another prayer answered, another victory won!

By the time our daughter would reach kindergarten, we would have had two more exploratory surgeries to make sure everything was okay, and at this point she was considered cured. We would find out that she was also born with no enamel on her baby teeth. So a lot of her teeth were literally like chalk and had to be pulled. She also was found to be predominantly blind in her left eye and her right eye wasn't much better. There would be many dental visits, glasses, patches and finally contact lenses at the age of nine. Other than that, she is a healthy and happy little girl. When I questioned why all these things had happened to her, they said it could have been due to the cancer surgery that I had had when I was pregnant with her, and the fact that she was not completely developed when the surgery occurred.

At this point in my life, I am a little older, a little wiser, and I'm realizing that there is more to my life than just living. As I began to pray about the purpose of my life, God began to reveal a greater plan and, that He would help me take steps in that direction. I had been teaching Sunday school for quite a while now and I felt that God was calling me to do more. The children's pastor at the church asked me to consider a leadership position. I told him I would pray about it and get back to him. It was at this time in my life that I would realize that when God calls you into the ministry, opposition comes with a vengeance.

My mother and I were barely speaking to each other, it was an on-again-off-again relationship. It was hard for me to talk with her, especially about God. As I was trying to make a decision whether to go into ministry or not, I wanted approval, her approval; I thought that maybe she would be proud of me for choosing this path. When I called her, I proceeded to make small talk, and as the conversation evolved, I told her about the decision I was facing. The response that came next shocked me. Just when you think you can't be shocked anymore, you are. She proceeded to tell me that I was the biggest "screw up" of her life. To this day, she denies saying it, but my heart and ears knows what I heard. When I hung up, my heart was shattered. Why did I even bother?

I talked with my husband and, after much prayer, I decided to take the position. I worked for the church in a volunteer position for about a year; thereafter, I was offered a staff position as the early childhood ministry director. I was very excited about what God was doing in my life and in my family's lives as well. Soon after I accepted this position, the children's pastor resigned and I was offered that position. With over ten years of experience working with children, God and I were able to do great things. I became an advocate for the children and did the very best I could in developing and designing programs that would teach them that being a Christian is not only cool, but fun. I made sure that they knew how special and loved they were. The children's ministry would grow and flourish greatly during this time.

About two years before my resignation, I felt that God was telling me to write a book. I thought to myself, *that would be cool, to write a book.* So I wrote one. Actually, I wrote a complete two-year preschool program for moms to home school their preschoolers. I had taken everything I had taught in my daycare and preschool and put it on paper. However, this was not the type of book God was talking about, and I knew this. But, I couldn't see myself, at that time, writing a book about my life. For one thing it was too painful. As my life went on, this issue was like a headache that wouldn't go away. Every time I would testify, people would say, "You should write a book." God was confirming this task every time I turned around. Finally, I gave in and began to write.

In March of 2000, I had to make the painful decision to resign from the church. I felt God was moving me to the next level in my life and I knew that if I stayed in my position, I wouldn't write this book. It was very difficult for me. I loved the children, and I loved my job. It would have been too difficult to try and do both as well as raise my family.

About a year before my resignation, I had been praying about my purpose. We knew that we were supposed to make a move, but we were not sure where. As we prayed, Texas kept coming to mind, so I researched everything we could think of about Texas, and after much prayer, we decided to move there. It seemed that as soon as we made the decision, doors began to open at every turn. My husband literally had half a dozen interviews lined up before he ever left Washington. Even though we were sad to leave, God completely blessed us for our obedience. He left in June to get everything ready, and the kids and I left the first week in July. We traveled all summer and had a blast seeing some of God's greatest wonders and beauties. Our first stop was California; we visited my husband's parents before heading to Yosemite to see El Capitan, and then on to my mom's house in the San Bernardino Mountains. From there we went to the Grand Canyon. It was a great trip! We pulled into San Antonio, Texas the second week of August. My husband had everything ready for us—a nice apartment with a pool and playground for the kids. He took a job with a popular restaurant chain making more money than he did in Seattle. God was blessing us and life was looking good.

We found a great church and began to settle into Texas life. The kids started school, we had good jobs, and the book was coming right along. You always know when you are right where God wants you, because the Devil will try and play havoc on your life. Just as we were getting on our feet, our family's health would be attacked. This would be a year of heartache for us. Due to severe adhesions in my abdomen, as well as other problems, I had to have a complete hysterectomy in January of 2001, and my husband was diagnosed with diverticulitis a week after my surgery and was admitted to the hospital as well. Boy, we were a pair. Our poor children had to take care of us; I don't think they knew what to think. However, God healed us both in short order. After a few days, my husband was back to work; it took a few weeks for me to return.

Our lives would be turned upside down as our baby daughter began to have urinary tract infections, again. This was confusing to us because she hadn't really had any problems for so long. Her pediatrician referred us to a pediatric urologist and we were off and running once more. They performed the usual tests, and found that one of the tubes that had been reconstructed literally unraveled and that she would be facing major surgery one more time. I was devastated; I thought we had conquered this problem once and for all.

Because the infections were so bad, they opted for surgery right away. Within a couple of weeks we found ourselves in that familiar situation of five years earlier. I can honestly tell you that most of my gray hair was born in waiting rooms.

As if this wasn't enough, I had been scheduled for my once-a-year scan to maintain my cancer-free status around the same time. Because I had already started the radiation injections, it could not be postponed. The day after our daughter's surgery, I would find out the results of the scan. When my doctor entered the exam room, he said, "Mrs. Rizan, let's go to my office." My blood ran cold as I sat in the chair across the desk from him. He said, "We found a tumor in the same area of your neck as before. However," he said, "it is quite small, but we need to start treatment right away due to the aggressiveness of the last tumor." As I sat there looking at him, I said, "I'm a little confused, I thought that this cancer was highly treatable and curable. I was told, that after the last treatment in 1993, it would probably never return." The doctor said, "Well, usually in 95% of all cases, this is true." "So, in what percentage do I fall?" I asked. He said, "It appears that this cancer is stubborn, you may fall in that 5% category." I just said, "When do we start treatment?"

When I reached the parking lot, I just started laughing hysterically. I'm sure that there are a few people who probably thought I was crazy, but I couldn't help it. I just kept thinking, *Who does this happen to? This is insane!* I looked up toward Heaven and said, "I don't want to do this anymore?" I just didn't understand.

As I headed back to the children's hospital, I began to pray and ask God for the strength to smile and not cry, and I asked Him for the strength to get me through this one more time. Again, I couldn't help but look at the irony of this situation. The very disease, in me, that caused my daughter to have all of the problems she faced was back, and how ironic that at the same time she had to face surgery, I had to face treatment, again. It appeared that we both would be fighting for our lives one more time.

When I arrived at the hospital, I didn't tell anyone about my test results, I just wanted to focus on my daughter. It wasn't until much later that evening that I told my husband. We cried, what else could we do? Our stress level was being tested.

The surgery on my daughter would prove to be a great success and easier than before, due to only one tube needing to be repaired. Our daughter healed beautifully and the news from the doctor was very encouraging. As time went on, she would have only one infection in a year and a half. Once again, she is considered healed. Praise God!

My radiation treatment was scheduled a few weeks after my daughter's surgery. My doctor was confident that because we had caught the tumor early, the radiation treatment would be more than adequate. I checked into the hospital and waited for the doctor to bring my treatment. The surroundings were more familiar than I was comfortable with. Plastic covered everything and those wonderful hospital gowns with the built in air conditioners were almost more than I could take. I have tried to find humor in every situation. I find that it tends to keep the attitude light and promotes quicker healing, although, it was difficult to find the humor here.

My doctor entered the room, and this time, the treatment was a pill not a drink—this was definitely better than before. The dose wasn't as large as the one I had received in 1993, but my doctor felt that it was adequate. The radiation emitted from my body fairly quickly this time, and because of this I didn't have to be in isolation as long. However, the rules still applied when I went home: Stay ten feet away from the kids, can't sleep in the same bed as my husband, the couch wrapped in plastic, rinse the shower twice, flush twice, wash my clothes at least three times, disposable toothbrushes, disposable plates, cups and plastic-ware. This time it wasn't as bad for my kids because they were old enough to understand, but it was still a little frightening for them.

As we lived out the next year of our lives, we were optimistic for the future. The one thing I knew for sure, at this point in my life, is that God is in control. I knew that He had a plan for all things and I had to believe that this was part of it. I love The Lord with all my heart and I knew that no matter what, I would live my life for Him. I struggled with questions as we all do, and as I always had. God would answer those questions time after time, by showing me how the situation had helped or was going to help someone else. Now I'm no martyr and certainly don't want to be, but I know that everything we go through in our lives, whether it is good or not so good, we can turn it around and help others, if we choose. There are so many people who want to give up or wallow in self-pity. I am here to tell you that you can withstand anything as long as you have God on your side.

Often times, I have felt like Job, and many times I have envisioned the conversation that must have gone on between God and the Devil. I think it went something like this: The devil saw that Job was a good and faithful servant and he decided that he would prove to God that a little adversity would turn Job against Him. So, he convinced God to let him bring on the trials. After contemplating the situation, God said, "Okay, you can bring on the trials, but you can't have his life." So Satan went on his way and caused all these horrible things to happen to Job, emotionally and physically. His family and friends all turned on him. But you know what? Job did not turn away from God. Yes, he questioned Him and complained quite a bit, but he didn't turn away. When the trials were over, God blessed him even more than he had previously. God wants us to see that He would and still does prevail over the enemy. Now, this is my interpretation, of course. Please don't hesitate to read "The Book of Job" for your own interpretation.

There were times I felt God was against me, as was my family, friends, and "well-wishers" as they told me, "If you just had enough faith," or "You are being punished for past sins." If

I had continued to listen to the negative things people had said, I know I wouldn't be where I am. If I had given up, or continued to lean on my own understanding, I am sure I wouldn't be alive today. God has a way of making things better than they were before, just like in the story of Job. Satan may try and steal your joy by bringing on the trials; you have to remember that God is God and that in the end He always wins, and when He does, He will always make sure you win, too.

The trials that I face now are different; different because I have the peace of God in my heart, and I understand that in spite of the circumstances, He will get me through. Not only will He get me through, but He will show all concerned and beyond that He is a sovereign God who keeps His promises. He has made several to me and He has kept every one.

In October of 2002, I would have yet another opportunity to question and trust Him. Only this time, it would be a different kind of question. As I returned to the doctor for a check-up, we went through the normal exam and blood tests. When the results came back, they would be questionable. The doctor explained that the cancer marker in my blood was high and that he needed to run some more tests. They scheduled me for an MRI of the head and neck; however, when the results of that test returned, it showed a tumor in the neck and some shadowing in the shoulder area. So they scheduled a CAT scan of the head, neck and upper part of the chest. When those results came back, it showed not only a tumor in the neck, but one under the clavicle and some shadowing in the chest area. Now I have to tell you that I was becoming a little more than anxious at this point. I knew that if I had cancer in my lungs that my chances for survival didn't look good. They ordered yet another test called a PET scan. This test would scan my whole body; if there was cancer to be found anywhere, this test would find it.

When we got the results back, they were both good and bad. They had confirmed the tumor in the neck and under the clavicle, but also confirmed was two masses in the aortic arch near the main pulmonary artery. They couldn't be sure if the tumor was attached to the outside or the inside of the aorta. Needless to say, we were less than pleased with the results; however, the good news is that these were the only tumors they found. There was nothing in the lungs or the rest of my body, and for this, I was grateful.

As we discussed treatment, my doctor said that surgery was eminent. My next appointment was with a cardio thoracic surgeon. He was a little taken back by the situation as well as my history. His reaction was, "We just don't see people like you." In other words he felt, as many doctors had, that I should not be alive given my medical history. He was amazed to say the least. A lot of doctors in the past wanted to know every detail of my medical history, they wanted to know why I had made it when others hadn't. I knew why, and my answer to them was always the same: "I have a very strong faith," and they agreed that it had to be.

He explained that he would have to crack the chest, as if I were having open-heart surgery, in order to remove the tumors. He would then go into the neck and clavicle and remove those tumors as well. Before closing, he explained that he would do exploratory surgery to make sure he had gotten everything, and to make sure that everything else was as it should be. I don't think I breathed very much during that appointment. I wasn't scared; I felt a little inconvenienced. I knew how long it took to recover from a surgery like this, and I didn't relish the fact that so much of my life would be spent recovering on a couch or bed.

The date was set, and from the time they found the cancer to the time of the surgery date was about three weeks. One of the things I have always been blessed with is great doctors. Because of my history, they didn't mess around; they took care of the problem right away. Early detection is also a plus. If I thought that something was wrong, praise God. He gave me the sense to see a doctor. You know a lot of people think that a miracle is only when God does something outrageous or out of the blue. This is not true, whether you get healing from a doctor's intervention or from divine intervention, it doesn't matter; it's still a miracle of God. I tell people all the time, "Whom do you think gave the doctor their brain?" If it weren't for God, nothing would be possible; that's why we know that with God, all things are possible!

During this time, I had a lot of time to talk with God about this situation and I didn't question Him in the way I had in the past. I wanted to know if I had missed Him somewhere along the way. I felt that He had made promises concerning my life, and I wanted to know if I had misinterpreted them. One day I was shopping when I saw a grandmother with her grandchildren, and emotion took hold of my heart. I commented to God that I wanted to see my grandchildren who weren't even born yet. He gently touched my heart and said, "You will see your grandchildren." I was very happy at this answer; it brought tears to my eyes and joy to my heart. However, you have to understand how my mind works. I said, "Okay, God, but could you please clarify your answer and tell me if I will see them first on earth or in Heaven?" I am almost positive that God was rolling in laughter. You know, a lot of people think that God doesn't talk to us anymore, that He only talked to people in biblical times. I am here to tell you that He does talk to us. It may not be in an audible voice, but He touches our hearts and we just know. He gives us that confidence and peace that we can't explain or understand, we just know. Hello! This is God talking, don't put Him off and don't analyze it to death, just listen. I would always add the "yeah but" to my sentences, don't make that mistake, just let God speak and hear Him when He does.

The day came for the surgery, and this would be the day I received the answer to my question. Had I misinterpreted God? It was simple: if I woke up on earth, I had not misinterpreted Him; I was okay either way. I think this was the calmest I had ever been going into surgery. My mom and stepfather had made the trip to be with me as well. The waiting room would be full as our pastor, his wife, and friends from our church, as well as family would be there, all praying for my recovery. God is so good; it is much harder on the family when illness strikes a member than on the person who is ill, this is my opinion. A lot of times I think they need more prayer than the person who is ill. Once I go to the operating room, I'm asleep through it all. They, on the other hand, have the most stressful task of all, sitting and waiting.

The surgery was supposed to take about three hours; it only took two. The doctor came out and told my husband that everything went fine and I was on my way to recovery. He said that he felt like he got all the cancer, and that they had sent the tumors to pathology to be tested. We wouldn't know exactly what we were dealing with or what the course of treatment would be until the results came back. They didn't know if I still had thyroid cancer or whether there may be a secondary cancer in my system. The doctor did tell us that the tumor they took out of the neck and clavicle were obviously malignant; however, he wasn't sure about the ones in my chest. He also informed us that the tumors in the neck and clavicle were small, but the one in the chest was as big as his fist and about an inch thick. We would just have to wait and see.

When I woke up in recovery, I looked around and my first thought was, *This is not Heaven.* The answer to my question was clear, and so was the pain in my chest. I have never felt physical pain like that before. They gave me a little button that was attached to a morphine pump and I knew that this was going to be my best friend for a while.

The next day, I was moved from intensive care to a regular room without incident. Four days after surgery, I was released to go home, where for the next four weeks I would recover before I was to begin treatment.

About a week later, we received the results of the pathology test. The tumor in the neck and clavicle were malignant, but the tumors in the chest were benign. What a victory! The doctors were worried more about the chest area than the other two, as the results could have been devastating had they come back with a malignancy. Now we knew what we were dealing with: Follicular Thyroid Carcinoma. This radiation treatment would be the highest level I would receive thus far.

The day came for the treatment, and once again the scene was all too familiar. This treatment would leave me very sick and weak. My doctor said that because of the surgery my body was basically torn apart and that it would take some time to completely recover.

It was time to go home once again, and all the old rules applied: stay ten feet away from the kids, can't sleep in the same bed as my husband, the couch wrapped in plastic, rinse the shower twice, flush twice, wash clothes at least three times, disposable toothbrushes, disposable plates, cups and plastic-ware.

It's over! Another battle won, time to get on with life!

Life continues to move rapidly, and as a result relationships either become closer or more distant. This time in my life marks a great milestone. My parents invited the kids and I to California to spend some time at their summer home. We decided to go, it was a welcomed vacation and I was able to spend time with my sister, brother, and parents. I was a little apprehensive, but ready to once and for all heal this part of my life.

As we visited, the time was very relaxing with swimming, fishing, boating, cooking, eating and just being a family. This was very nice, tranquility at its very best. One night after dinner, the conversation took a turn to the past. My sister had been dealing with the pain of our biological father for many months now and she, too, was ready to resolve issues within our family. As we began to talk about it, my mom became very defensive, as she felt guilty that she had not believed me years ago and that she didn't take us with her when she left, and we were trying frantically to console her. We were not here to pass blame or judgment, we just wanted to be a family. My mom got up to leave, hurt, and we followed her; we were not going to let this opportunity pass by. If we had, our family would not be able to heal. My brother intervened and said very sternly that we would talk, and we did. For hours we talked and the resolution emerged, as did our family. This was a time of cleansing and great healing. Since this time, the relationship between my mother and I has only gotten better—she is my mom and I love her very much. Amazingly, life has a way of continuing, with or without you. So much time wasted in bitterness and unforgiveness, so much hurt and anger. The relationship with my mother has, to say the least, been a love-hate relationship. If you could see us now—what would you see? You would see a mother and a daughter who have waited so long to love each other. You would see a relationship that has gone from a thorny bush to a beautiful bouquet, with love and respect restored. I am sure you have heard the phrase that "Hurting people hurt people." This has been a classic case, but no more. It hasn't all been easy, but we continue to work on it. I accept her for who she is as she does with me. I have also learned a lot about the cloth in which I was cut and I am proud to be a part of my mother's cloth. I think that age, time, maturity and wisdom have fallen on this family and we realize all that we have missed and we realize what we don't want to miss. God has restored this relationship and I am grateful and amazed by what He has done. Mom, I love you!

May 2004, I find myself once again in the doctor's office for my one-year exam to determine if I am cancer free. The scan came back clean. As I hear these words, I feel my knees give way and my doctor rushes to help me. We were both emotional and so happy. My doctor tells me that just one more test is needed, my blood work. Once this test is confirmed, it will be official—cancer free!

I anxiously await the call. Finally, it comes, but the words on the other end of the phone are ones of sorrow and sadness. I can't believe what I am hearing. The cancer marker is up and we must begin the search of where it has now tried to plant itself. My doctor makes the necessary arrangements for a PET scan. This time we will go straight for the most conclusive test possible.

The results are in and my doctor is told to tell me to prepare myself and my family for the results. When my doctor receives this news, his reaction is confused; this is not possible, it has to be a mistake. This type of cancer does not do this, and the cancer marker is not high enough to support their findings.

I had been sick a few weeks earlier and had to receive two rounds of antibiotics for what we thought was strep throat as well as a bacterial infection. What they didn't tell my doctor was that I had to be well and off the antibiotics for at least four weeks prior to taking this scan. So when the scan was complete, I lit up like a Christmas tree. They thought I was dying right then. My doctor brought me into the office to tell me the news.

I was not happy, and it also put many questions and doubts into my mind. "What if the test is not wrong?" He assured me that it was. He knew the cancer was back, he just didn't know where it was, and that alone is enough to set you on edge. He set up an ultra-sound, which he performed himself. This doctor is amazing, he was fighting for me and he knew that he was going to find it no matter where it was, and he did. The ultra-sound was performed in the neck area since this has always been the source; it would make sense to start there. He found it and it was the size of a tiny bead. "Now," he said, "we'll biopsy it and find out what is going on." He scheduled a biopsy for later and again he performed it himself. Something that tiny, it would be a challenge to biopsy. Once again, after several tries, he gets what he needs and now enough time has passed to perform other tests so we can see the magnitude of this cancer. I was scheduled for another PET scan and it came back positive for tumors in the lymph nodes of the neck, but also, it was showing a mass around the left kidney and adrenal gland as well. So he ordered an MRI, with and without contrast, to figure out exactly what was going on. I was told that if there was cancer in or around the kidney and adrenal gland that it was most likely a secondary cancer. It wouldn't be the Follicular Carcinoma. Needless to say, my mind went hurling once again. Why? Why? Why?

Because of my history and the nature of this cancer, they superimposed the kidney and adrenal area to get the best possible look. They had shown me on the PET scan, prior to the MRI, the mass that they were looking at. It was there, I saw it, the written report revealed it, and it made me very nervous. However, when the results of the MRI came in, it was gone—nowhere to be found! Prayer? Oh yeah. Answer to prayer? Oh yeah!

We still had to deal with the cancer in the neck, but at least we knew where it was now and what type, and most likely what kind of treatment. My doctor makes an appointment with a head and neck surgeon and we are off and running.

Sitting in the waiting room always makes me feel sick to my stomach, even though I know what's going on and what they are going to do. I gave up a long time ago trying to read a magazine and get my mind off the situation; I would just rather hit it head on with full steam and get it over with. I wasn't scared, I was angry and hurt—the full range of emotions that always come with this sort of news. It doesn't take me long to get past those feelings now, though. I just go on and do what I need to do. I got past being fearful a while ago. I know God is in control, and I know He hasn't brought me this far just to let me go that easy—not a chance, He has too much work for me to do.

It is too bad you can't have the same surgeon for everything. As the nurse calls me in we make small talk and I belt out with some cheesy humor. She laughs and says, "The doctor will be right with you." So I wait, he enters and we begin to talk. He has already been briefed on my history and, as many others are, is pretty amazed that I am sitting there speaking, understanding, and alertly looking at him. He proceeded to explain the procedure, which quite frankly took my breath away. The incision would literally go from one ear to the next, and he was very truthful about that. He also said that he would do everything he could to save my voice, but there were no guarantees. He said that one time of scraping the vocal cord nerve was one thing, but twice? He said he would do all he could. Again, my calling hinges on speaking and singing, so I had no choice but to believe and have faith that God would indeed see me through this once again. I had my reservations and cried out to God to give me peace that all would be well.

The day came for surgery, my spirits were high; I just wanted it to be over. My doctor came in and again I pleaded with him about my voice. I told him that I speak, and that my girls and I sing Christian music, I needed my voice. "No promises," he said, "but I'll do all I can." He smiled as he turned and walked away. The surgery took a couple of hours and they took out forty-three lymph nodes, twenty from the right side all benign, nineteen from the left side, one malignant. He found tumors in four lymph nodes along the trachea, all malignant. He scraped the vocal cord nerve, looked around to make sure there was nothing else, and got out. The surgery went well and I headed for recovery.

When I woke up, I remember putting my hands up to my face and saying to God, "Okay, here we go." As I opened my mouth to speak, tears began to flow. God had spared my voice, another victory, another miracle. The doctor told me that he has done many if not hundreds of these surgeries but not once has he seen happen to anyone what happened to me in this situation. He said that when he cut me the vocal cord nerve was laying right there on top as if to say, "Here I am, see me, don't hurt me." His words: "You must have had someone looking out for you." He said usually they have to search for it and by the time they find it, it is too late. Feel the miracle? I sure do!

Time for healing and time to get ready for treatment. The old familiar scene begins to emerge; radiation treatment at the highest level thus far would be the way to go.

As I prepare for treatment, an illumination of dread falls on my mind. The time it takes to get the body prepped to receive the radiation treatment is grueling. After surgery, I usually get a couple of weeks to recover. When the doctor feels recovery is well on its way, I am taken off my thyroid medication. The thyroid regulates your energy level as well as your metabolism and other pertinent chemicals that make you feel like a thriving human being. The key is to throw your body into "hypothyroidism;" in other words, starve your body of iodine. The treatment for thyroid cancer is radioactive iodine, and the theory goes so that when the radiation is administered, your body is so starved for the iodine that it soaks it up as fast as it can, thus, the radiation kills any left over cancer cells. However, getting your body to the point of iodine starvation is quite a task. The longer you stay off the thyroid medication the more side effects emerge, such as weight gain, excessive water retention, swelling, sensitivity to sound, ears ringing, muscle weakness and fatigue, overwhelming tiredness, insomnia, irritability, impatience and intolerance to the simplest of tasks and situations, overwhelming emotions, feeling like you can't function or cope—basically you just don't feel like a person. The whole process from surgery to prepping the body to the treatment takes about six to eight weeks. After treatment, and from the day you start back on your medication, it takes about two months to get your blood levels regulated to the point that you feel like you're really back among the living. It is quite an undertaking and I have to say, not something that I look forward to. I am not the only one to suffer. My family goes through the preparation and treatment right along with me. This is not the mother they are used to having around and it is very hard on them to make this temporary adjustment. The key for me to overcome is keeping a positive attitude and, more importantly, having an utmost reliance on the faith that God will get me through.

This is where my healing has come. Negativity has no place in the lives of those that are afflicted. I'm not talking about denial, or just not facing it, I am a firm believer in identifying the problem—educating yourself and then facing it head on with prayerful guidance. This doesn't mean that you can't feel bad or complain, Lord knows I've done enough of that, but; don't let it overtake you. You are a champion, you are the head and not the tail, you are above and not beneath, you can do all things through Christ Jesus who strengthens you. God knows we are human, and He knows that we need Him; it is up to us to cry out for help. It is up to us to choose Him, which is what He is waiting for. Cover the illness with prayer and the word and let God do the healing. Whether it be through doctors or divine healing, a miracle is a miracle, God is in control of *ALL* miracles.

This treatment by far was the worst one; the dosage was higher, and I felt as though I could die. The nausea, the swelling, I kept looking at the clock, counting down the hours of the day, knowing that if I made it through to the next day, that that would be one less day to suffer. By the time I left the hospital, I was unrecognizable. The radiation had set in my glands and the swelling was overwhelming. My eyelids looked like fluid-filled balloons and my eyes were little slits to see out of. Destination—home. Upon my arrival, all the old rules applied: stay ten feet away from the kids, the couch wrapped in plastic, rinse the shower twice, flush twice, wash clothes at least three times, disposable toothbrushes, disposable plates, cups and plastic-ware.

As I embark on the last words of this book, my life is by no means over, and I am sure I will have the opportunity to keep you informed on how this life is progressing. I don't know what will happen now, I have to believe that I am healed, and in my heart I am. Twelve months from now the results will be in, until then I have to keep believing and praying, all the while doing God's work.

I know that my life has a long way to go and I am ready to live it. I will constantly have to work on relationships in my life, as well as continue to forgive the wrongs of others and repent for the wrongs I do, and will do. But, it has been quite a life so far. What I have shared with you are glimpses; please understand that there is so much more. I sit here humbled at the opportunity to live. Knowing that God loves me so much that He would rescue me from, what we deem as, the injustices of life, you can look at this like a super hero story. There is a villain, a victim, and a hero. The dark side tried to prevail; however, there is not enough darkness in this world to drown out the light of goodness. God is my hero, and as you can see, He has rescued me from a lot and I know that as I continue to live out the rest of my life, he will continue to make me the victor and not the victim.

A lot of tears and agony literally went into the writing of this book. It took almost six years to complete and I had to take quite a few breaks because of the constant reliving of some of the most rewarding, yet painful, parts of my life. The promise is what got me through. My calling is to help those who are hurting. God promised that this book would help to heal the hearts of others and this is what gave me the strength to write. You know, everyone has a testimony or story, if you will. You may think that yours is unimportant or insignificant but you're wrong. The things that you are going through are just as important and traumatic as mine or anyone else's, because you are going through them. Who's to say whose are better or worse? I just know that God is there to help anyone who will call upon His name. He helped me and He can help you.

I have been through many things: sexual, physical and verbal abuse, abandonment, divorce, the loss of three children, fourteen major surgeries, cancer four times, not to mention the emotional wear and tear. At the age of 38, my body looks like a jigsaw puzzle. All this life before the age of 39, and I still have a lot of life to live, and I can't wait, because I know that from here on out, it can only get better.

I can honestly tell you that the joys of life far outweigh the grief. Things that we all take for granted like looking at the sky and wondering how it got so blue, or why the ocean seems to be endless and free, or the beauty of a sunset. Looking into the eyes of a newborn baby and being amazed by creation; answering the constant whys of a five-year-old and realizing that in their eyes you are the greatest thing in the world. What about feeling true love? Or seeing how your children are growing into awesome individuals, knowing that you are the one who has helped them get there? Oh yes, life is good because Jesus Christ lives! He lives in me and that, my friend, is what got me this far and will continue to get me through the next 38 plus years.

I have found the treasure in my attic, and my prayer is that you, too, will find the treasure in yours.

If you are interested in a guest speaking, a special appearance booking, or a book signing, contact Tammie Rizan at:

treasureintheattic2005@hotmail.com

LaVergne, TN USA
17 December 2010
209194LV00001B/4/P

9 781413 761993